CW00404003

The A-Z of Practical Self-Sufficiency

By Carl May & Kal Horsfall

THE A-Z OF PRACTICAL SELF-SUFFICIENCY

Published by The Good Life Press Ltd. 2011

Text copyright © Carl May & Kal Horsfall
www.attainableselfsufficiency.co.uk

All rights reserved. No parts of this publication, including text or illustrations, may be reproduced or stored in a retrieval system, or transmitted, in any form or by any means, electronic, mechanical, photocopying, recording or otherwise, without prior permission of the publisher, The Good Life Press Ltd.

ISBN 978-1907866036

A catalogue record for this book is available from the British Library.

Published by
The Good Life Press Ltd.
PO Box 536
Preston
PR2 9ZY

www.goodlifepress.co.uk
www.homefarmer.co.uk

Contents

FOREWORD

At some point in our lives, most of us will experience the need or desire to change the way we live. It may be down to a life-changing event, or simply a gnawing feeling that there must be a better way. For some this thought will be a fleeting moment, but for others it will be the start of a journey to find a better way of life.

Whatever the ills of our modern age, we are without doubt better off than previous generations. Better education, healthcare and a basic standard of living mean that we are living longer and have more say in how we lead our lives. No longer confined by rigid social values we now have the freedom to change our lives, no matter how difficult that change may be.

It's this ability to choose how we live that is perhaps the starting point of this book. No, we can't throw in our jobs straight away, and no we can't stop paying our bills but what we can do is to think and plan about how we can make our lives more fulfilling.

Our idea of 'practical self-sufficiency' is just that – taking the best bits of life and enjoying all the advantages of the modern age, but moulding the rest of our lives into something less frantic. We can't claim to be self-sufficient, but what we have is a way of life that we can control.

We want this book to be a first-step reference book for those like-minded souls who realise that total self-sufficiency is almost impossible, and who also may be put off by the thought of turning their garden into a small zoo (although that may still come later!). You don't need to start with a huge allotment, or even live in the country; you just need a desire to re-evaluate all the elements that affect your life on a day-to-day basis.

We shall cover a wide range of topics, starting with ideas on how you can begin to plan to change your life. We shall try to pass on useful practical skills and tips that have helped us, and also how to budget your outgoings, turn the contents of your fridge into a superb meal, and how to make money from your plot.

Most of all, we want you to enjoy your journey. It may take time, but look at it as being just as important as attaining your goal, so try to embrace all the chapters along the way.

Finally, we we have provided website addresses and phone numbers wherever possible. We apologise in advance for where only website addresses are given. This is because these services are only available online

ALLOTMENTS

.Many of you may already have a 'patch' of land with your dwelling. Whether this is a long, narrow stretch at the back of an old-fashioned terraced house or a more conventional shape and sized garden, you will already have the ability to grow crops to at least some extent.

However, some of you may want to grow but might not be fortunate enough to have a patch of land outside your back door, or you may want a bit more space. There are a few ways to overcome this situation:

- *Growing on a neighbour's patch who may not be able to tend their land*
- *Running a small micro garden in pots and planters (see the garden chapter)*
- *Getting involved in either school or neighbourhood projects*
- *Renting yourself an allotment*

An allotment could be the answer and it will give you much in return by

- *producing great things to eat*
- *keeping you fit*
- *reducing stress*
- *making new friends*

FINDING AND CHOOSING A PLOT

Every Council will have a different approach and level of availability when it comes to finding a plot. It's not possible to state the exact way which may be right for you, but we have listed some useful avenues to start you off in the right direction.

First and foremost, contact your local Council and find out how many allotments they have, where they are, and crucially, the waiting list. Don't despair if they tell you that you have more chance of beating Beelzebub in a snowball competition than getting a plot as there are other ways.

Many landowners rent out plots privately.
Scour through local maps to find available plots.
Ask existing plot holders. On Council plots they may be able to tell you of any up and coming sites.
Speak to your local librarian who may be able to help.
Go online as many private allotments have websites and you can gain useful information from them.

If all else fails there is one last final and little known way in which your Council can help you. Everyone has a legal right to an allotment under the 1908 Smallholdings and Allotments Act. It is there in case a situation arises where demand greatly outstrips supply, and requires the provision of additional plots should six or more people on the electoral roll put their case forward in writing. Laws are, however, being changed daily, so for more up to the minute details go to **www.legislation. gov.uk** and search for the Act. If this is a last resort then I wish you good luck.

Once you have located an allotment with a vacant plot(s), take some time to consider its worthiness before you jump in with both wellies.

HOW CLOSE IS IT TO HOME?

You may not be able to pick and choose, but if the plot you are considering is some considerable distance from your house then think of the reality of driving out there on a regular basis on wet days with a boot full of tools, compost and crops.

EASY ACCESS

As a newcomer, try not to get a corner plot as this will not only greatly increase the distance you have to carry everything to and from your car, but it may also isolate you from the very people you may come to rely on for assistance. Think about pathways and how easy it is to get to and from the plot. Make sure you are close to a water supply too as some sites do not allow hose pipes, and walking

backwards and forwards in summer laden with heavy watering cans will very soon become a nuisance.

CONDITION

Look for a plot that is as level as possible to avoid terracing or soil slippage. Try to find a south-facing aspect to maximise the amount of sun.

Look at the condition of the plot. It may have been left unattended for many months and, although the thought of starting from the beginning can seem like a good idea at the outset, it could soon prove to be an incredible amount of hard work.

Look for deep, rich, well-composted soil to confirm that it has been well fed and looked after in the past.

AMENITIES

Find out if the plot has a shed, fruit cages, or compost bins. Speak to other plot holders to get a real feel for the lie of the land. Do they have a toilet onsite? Find out the particular rules and dos and don'ts that will affect you, and make sure that you keep to them.

SIZE IS IMPORTANT

Plots are measured and sub-divided into perches, poles, or rods. It gets a bit confusing for the novice, but as a rule of thumb most plots are around 253 square meters, about the size of a tennis court. They are then sometimes sub-divided into half plots.

Be realistic. If you are offered a full-sized plot, get friends and family to help in looking after it. Eagerness from the outset can become an encumbrance later on when you find you have too much space and not enough time or energy.

WHEN?

The best time to take on your new patch would be in autumn or early winter. This will give you plenty of time to prepare the ground for sowing the following year. It will also stop a frantic rush in early spring to get all your tasks completed before planting.

WHAT TO DO NEXT

So, you have your plot and you don't know where to start. Begin by drawning up a plan. Think about what you want to grow and how much of it you will need. Look at the style of gardening you want to do, whether open or raised beds etc. (see Garden Skills, Chapter 7).

The effort required to clear the plot will of course depend on its condition, but spend some time getting the site clear, creating defined paths, a compost area, and perhaps space for a shed, greenhouse or polytunnel, if one does not already exist.

Make sure you have good storage space (a shed or at least a large storage box) that is sound, weather proof, and above all secure. If you have a shed, fit guttering and a water butt to save water and never-ending journeys to the tap.

So good luck in finding the right allotment for you. There are many useful websites such as **www.allotment.org.uk** that can help you further.

BUDGETING

When any of us are considering a life change it requires an immense amount of thought and planning. It's often said that simply having a dream can increase the likelihood of that dream coming true, but it also needs a personal determination to turn that dream into a reality.

One of the first areas you will need to tackle is to take a good and honest look at just how you stand financially. Draw up a budget plan and complete it with total honesty. If you have any debts then now is the time to total them up and take advice on the best way of clearing them.

By working through your budget plan you will see how much you need to earn each month, and what kind of things you could perhaps do without or pay a better price for. You will really find looking at your finances in black and white an illuminating process!

We'll also look at ways you can reduce your grocery bills. You can use a larder stock sheet to help you with menu planning and storing food. There's also a section on reducing utility bills (see Chapter 5), plus cutting the cost of your household purchasing, and Chapter 3 on homemade cleaning products will not only save you money, but you'll also be using fewer chemicals too!

Cutting The Cost Of Your Grocery Bills

CARRY OUT A LARDER AUDIT

One of the easiest ways to reduce your food bills is to create your own Larder Stock Sheet and plan to do a big shop once a fortnight. You will need to make a list of the meals you would like to cook during this time. Use the stock sheet to work out just what you will need to buy in order to feed your family for the whole of this period.

To begin with it will cost you extra money to set it up, but if you can manage this it's amazing how much you will save in the long term by not 'popping' out to the supermarket every few days!

9

The other advantage of doing this is that you can build up extra stock, so if you have a lean time in the future you will always have food in the house.

PLAN YOUR MEALS

If you make a list of the meals you want to eat, you'll know exactly what you need to buy, and you'll be far more focused when you do your shopping. Never buy 'ready meals' – they cost a fortune and taste like cardboard. Do your taste buds and wallet a favour and learn to cook!

CASH AND CALCULATOR

Always shop with a list. The old adage of not shopping when you're hungry is very true. Once you're into a routine with your Stock Sheet leave your debit cards at home and take only cash, and use your calculator if you need to. This will stop you buying any extras. Do budget in some treats though. No matter how tough things are an occasional bar of chocolate or a bottle of wine can ease the pain!

LEFTOVER FOOD

Don't forget to use leftovers. Wasting food is not only expensive but a terrible habit when you think of all the people going hungry in the world. Freeze leftovers once the food has cooled if you don't think you'll eat it the next day. Take a look at **www. lovefoodhatewaste.com** for some great recipe ideas.

FRUIT AND VEG

Never buy these pre-packed or pre-sliced, it will always cost you more. Buying in season is far better in monetary terms and food miles too, and don't buy snack packs as you get very little for your money. Store your fruit and veg properly so they last for longer.

Try your local market. You probably won't be able to buy enough fruit and veg to last a fortnight or a month, so this could be a good way of not going back into the supermarket!

FOOD SHOPPING ONLINE

Try doing your supermarket shop online. Once you've got your list you could visit **www.mysupermarket. co.uk** to check out which is the cheapest. Don't forget though that online prices are only a guide. This is because supermarkets make daily price changes and the price you pay will probably be set on the day of delivery, so you may end up paying more than the site suggests.

BUYING 'OWN BRANDS'

Try supermarket 'own brand' labels as they will probably be cheaper. Visit **www.supermarketownbrandguide. co.uk** for an informative site run by Mark Isark, a professional taster who scores products on quality of taste plus health and nutrition information.

ONLINE CASH-BACK SITES

Earn money by doing your shopping through cash-back sites. Check out:

www.quidco.com

www.topcashback.co.uk

www.giveortake.com

www.rpoints.com

www.freefivers.co.uk

www.edeals.com

Whichever supermarket you use it's also worth checking out their website to see what deals they are doing, and if you haven't already done so then check out your local Aldi and Lidl. The quality of the food is very high and their prices are at least 20% cheaper than the main four supermarkets.

COUPONS AND VOUCHERS

There are also numerous voucher and coupon sites where you can print off discount vouchers to take with you next time you shop.

www.couponnet.co.uk

www.vouchercodes.com

www.myvouchercodes.co.uk www. freeinuk.co.uk

www.foodfreebies.co.uk

www.ukdiscountvouchers.co.uk

SUPERMARKET TIPS

- Only buy 'special offers' if you will use the items.
- Go to the back of the shelf to find the best 'use by' and 'best by' dates.
- Items in squeezy bottles are more expensive than glass bottles.
- Never buy from a petrol station shop; it will cost you a lot more.
- Try cheaper 'own brand' foods to see if you like the taste.

Away From The Supermarkets

BUY IN SEASON

In season fruit and veg will always be cheaper. If you're not sure what's currently in season there is an excellent website called **www. eattheseasons.co.uk** that tells you what food is in season. It also gives you tips on buying, storage, nutrition, and cooking.

MARKETS

Rediscover your local market. You can often get fresh local produce cheaper from a market. Some fruit and veg stalls will also discount their prices from around 3.30pm on a Saturday.

PICK YOUR OWN

Find your local pick-your-own farm. If you pick enough you can always freeze or bottle to preserve.

BUY LOCAL

Getting to know your local butcher

can help you save money. They'll be able to advise you on different cuts of meat and how to cook them. If you buy a larger quantity you may also be able to negotiate a discount. A good butcher will know too where his meat has come from, and in our opinion you will be buying far better tasting meat that you can buy from any supermarket.

www.bigbarn.co.uk is a great website for tracking down local food suppliers.

BUYING IN BULK

This requires some thought and planning. You will definitely need to know exactly what you need to buy, otherwise you will end up spending more than you planned. It's worth looking at supermarket value brand prices as well, especially if you're looking to buy the cheapest food items you can. Also make sure that you have enough space for storage, and that you can store food properly. This will mean investing in some good quality food storage containers.

If you have a business you will be able to join a cash and carry. The major ones include Makro, Booker and Costco. Don't forget to calculate the travelling cost to get to them. And also check to see if VAT is included on the label or added at point of sale, otherwise you may get bit of a surprise.

ETHICAL / ORGANIC BULK BUYING

If you prefer to buy organic or ethical food, start up a food group with some friends and buy in bulk. Check out:

www.sumawholesale.coop
www.infinityfoods.co.uk
www.naturallygoodfood.co.uk
www.ethicalsuperstore.co.uk

FARMERS' MARKETS

Buy direct from the producers for great quality food and drink. Using these markets keeps niche local businesses alive, and you'll know where your food has come from and how it has been prepared. Visit **www.farmersmarkets.net** for your nearest market, and **www.fork2fork.org.uk** also has information on buying local produce.

MISC.

www.approvedfoods.co.uk and **www.foodbargains.co.uk** are online retailers specialising in short-dated, out-of-date and clearance food and cleaning items.

MAKING SAVINGS WITH HOUSEHOLD PURCHASES

The Internet is a vast source of information and a valuable tool when it comes to saving money. The following are just a few of the available sites that may be of use to you:

CAR FUEL

www.petrolprices.com to find the cheapest fuel in your area.

HEATING OIL

Compare local heating oil prices on www.boilerjuice.com and www.whichoilsupplier.co.uk and look out for the buying weekends on the boilerjuice site.

BUYING WHITE GOODS

Unless you're really strapped for cash it's cheaper in the long run to buy new energy efficient electrical appliances. www.which.co.uk provides unbiased rundowns and comparisons on many items. www.appliancesonline.co.uk and www.appliancedeals.co.uk both offer good deals on white goods, together with free delivery.

www.clearance-comet.co.uk is an auction site for graded appliances. It works like eBay, but don't forget to factor in delivery costs of nearly £30.00 per item. At the time of writing Currys are also starting an online auction site.

You could try searching for 'ex-catalogue' freezers and fridges. www.find-electricalgoods.co.uk is an excellent site comparing the best prices of many electrical goods.

BOOKS, DVDS AND GAMES

www.find-book.co.uk will compare the prices of new books and www.find-dvd.co.uk compares both DVD and Blu-ray prices from major UK retailers. www.find-games.co.uk will find the cheapest deals on games, consoles, and accessories.

WINE

www.acaseofwine.co.uk has up-to-date information on promotions currently being offered by UK wine merchants.

EBAY

This site is a must if you are keeping an eye on your finances. You can also save by buying out of season. If you need to get another greenhouse, for example, try looking for it in October!

CLEANING PRODUCTS

If you want to cut the cost of cleaning, or would simply like to avoid using so many chemicals in your home, you could try making your own household cleaners. Make sure though that you don't use home-made cleaners with shop-bought products, and don't reuse old cleaner containers just in case they react with one another. Always label your containers with the date you made them and their ingredients.

We have found a fantastic website called **www.dri-pak.co.uk** which has loads of information on traditional cleaning and laundry products. You can also buy from their eBay shop.

WHITE VINEGAR

Being mildly acidic white vinegar will dissolve dirt, hard water deposits, and soap scum. It is also a natural deodoriser, absorbing smells rather than covering them up. Don't worry about your house smelling like a chip factory – once the vinegar has dried you won't smell it.

To clean the bath, shower, counter tops etc., simply dilute equal parts of vinegar and water in a spray bottle. For deeper cleaning leave the solution to sit for 20 to 30 minutes and then rinse off. For toilets use undiluted vinegar, leaving it again for 20 minutes, then scrub and rinse.

BICARBONATE OF SODA

This is non-toxic and can be used as an alternative to scouring powders or cream cleaners. Simply sprinkle some on a damp cloth or sponge and then wipe over. Alternatively, you can make it into a paste with water, apply and leave for 20 minutes, then rinse with water. This is useful for areas that need a bit of extra cleaning. It is suitable for cleaning most things except for marble surfaces.

Bicarbonate of soda also gets rid of perspiration odours, softens fabrics, and will remove some stains. Because it deodorises you can sprinkle it on carpets and pet bedding. Leave for 20 minutes and vacuum off. You may also want to try putting some small bowls of bicarbonate of soda around the home as an air freshener. It will also neutralise bee stings.

BORAX SUBSTITUTE

This can be bought from chemists, and is a deodoriser with antibacterial properties. It is gentler than soda crystals but stronger than bicarbonate of soda. In laundry washing borax substitute will soften water so that you don't need to use quite so much detergent. It also disinfects and deodorises, so it is very good for cloth nappies, pet bedding, and tea towels etc. Mixed with water and either lemon juice or white vinegar it makes a good multi-surface cleaner.

Borax is harmful if eaten, so don't use it where food is prepared, and keep it away from pets and children. It can also irritate the skin, so use gloves.

CLUB SODA

This is plain water into which carbon dioxide has been added, and it is great for removing stains from fabrics, upholstery, and carpets. It's also completely safe to use.

ESSENTIAL OILS

Tea tree, lemon, and eucalyptus are antibacterial. Lavender or orange will help to make a home smell nice. Use just a few drops when making up your home-made cleaning products.

Never ingest essential oils and, apart from tea tree and lavender, don't apply them directly onto skin.

HYDROGEN PEROXIDE

Hydrogen peroxide is a weak acid and comes in 3% or 6% dilution. It can be bought from chemists. It has antibacterial properties and is good for sanitising food preparation surfaces, light switches, toilets etc. It will also remove mould and mildew from tiles if sprayed on and left overnight. Don't buy in large quantities though or you may find yourself on the watch list of the anti-terrorist squad!

Simply spray hydrogen peroxide onto the surface you want to clean, leave it for at least two minutes and wipe. Only decant sufficient for your immediate requirements.

LIQUID CASTILE SOAP

This is made using olive oil and can be used for washing the dishes. Simply add some lemon essential oil. It can also be grated in water to hand wash items of clothing or mop the floor.

WASHING UP LIQUID

3 tbsp liquid Castile soap
2 cups warm water
2 tsp glycerine
2 tbsp white vinegar
10 drops lemon, orange or
lavender essential oil

15

Put all the ingredients in a jar, seal the lid and shake. Use about one tablespoon per bowl of dishes.

SALT

If you presoak clothing in salt water it will remove perspiration stains. Add equal quantities of salt, bicarbonate of soda and borax to make an all-purpose scouring agent.

Salt will remove tea and coffee stains, and if you make your own bread, rub salt onto the work surface to remove the bits of dough.

LEMONS

Lemons are acidic and will cut through grease. They are also antibacterial, so cut them in quarters and rub over chopping boards, work surfaces, cookers etc.

SODA CRYSTALS

Soda crystals are an alkaline chemical compound which can be bought from the laundry section of the supermarket and from the chemist. They do not contain any phosphates, enzymes, or bleach, and can be used to wash laundry and as a general all-purpose house cleaner, cleaning walls, floors, bathrooms etc. They are good for removing grease and will help to keep drains and sinks unblocked. You will need to wear gloves when using soda crystals, and never use them on aluminium or polished surfaces.

LAUNDRY GLOOP RECIPE

This recipe is for home-made laundry detergent, and should keep you going for a few weeks! Store it in several tubs, and don't use anything with a small opening as this recipe will solidify once it has cooled. To make it you will need:

A large stock pot with a tight fitting lid, and big enough to hold at least ten pints.
1 bar of unscented soap, grated
1cup or 250ml washing soda crystals
4 litres / 7 pints of water
20 drops essential oil

Bring the water to the boil, then turn down the heat, add grated soap, and stir in. Once it has dissolved completely turn off the heat and add the washing soda crystals. As soon as it has cooled add your essential oils and stir well. Decant into your containers.

Add about half a cup per wash, cutting up the gloop into small pieces and adding it directly into the drum of the machine. Do not put it into the drawer as the gloop may block the machine over time. Rinse the washing machine out by adding half a cup of white vinegar every so often to clean the machine. You can add the white vinegar to the rinse cycle with or without clothes inside.

HOME-MADE DISINFECTANT

You will need a spray bottle of white vinegar and a spray bottle of 3% hydrogen peroxide. Spray the surface to be cleaned with the hydrogen peroxide and then the vinegar. Rinse with water and allow to dry thoroughly. This will kill e-Coli, shigella and salmonella. Do not mix

these two products to store them as they can react with each other.

DIY SKILLS

One cost that hits nearly all households is that of repairing and refurbishing our homes, and in this chapter we are going to cover some basic DIY skills to help you 'have a go' and hopefully save some money along the way. If you are unsure about your DIY skills then start off by trying the little jobs to give you both practice and confidence.

In times of recession it is even more crucial to look after your dwelling, as selling is proving harder and harder. There are numerous super DIY stores that sell huge ranges of tools and gadgets aimed at the beginner to help him or her do just that. Before starting any job, try to get a sound understanding of the problem and how to fix it. The Internet is a great tool, or just ask a friend to show you.

As with most of life's skills DIY is best learnt starting with an understanding of the basic skills and the experience of giving it a go. What we want to cover here are the fundamentals and to highlight the tools and the skills you will need to tackle small tasks around the house. Some golden rules to start with are:

•   *Never carry out any work on electric wiring or fittings or gas piping and fixtures.*

•   *Use qualified professionals.*

•   *Never attempt structural work to your house. If you need to, always contact a reputable qualified builder.*

•   *If you are going to attempt any plumbing, make sure you know where the mains tap is.*

•   *If you are working on ladders always use the correct type, and make sure they are used in conjunction with the manufacturer's advice.*

•   *Give yourself plenty of time to get the job finished, and don't leave your house looking like a building site.*

BASIC TOOL KIT

Buying the best quality you can afford makes good sense, and this is especially applicable when buying a tool kit. There are many cheap alternatives to every tool you will need, but quality really will last, and will make the job easier to complete successfully.

Don't go out and buy the whole tool kit at once. Instead buy each tool when it's needed, but shop around and you could save a great deal of money. Remember to always clean and store your tools securely whenever you finish a job.

The following tool kit is in two parts; firstly the must haves, then the extras.

The Must Haves

Screwdrivers: both slotted and cross head, and 3 of each in various sizes.
Hammers: 1 heavy with a claw head and 1 lighter weight.
Saws: A 20 inch panel saw for cutting lengths and a tenon saw for joints and fine cuts.
Electric drill: cordless, if possible, and an assortment of drill bits for both wood and masonry.
Spirit level: 1 short and 1 long.
A Stanley knife
Pliers
A sealant gun
A tape measure
A scraper
A set of brushes 1", 1½", 2", 2½" and 3".

The Extras

A set of chisels
A carpenter's square for cutting straight lines.
A mitre block and saw for cutting accurate angles.
Trowels
An electric screwdriver
A cable detector to help locate cables and pipes in walls.
A plane
An electric sander
A vice

In reality the list is almost endless, but if you buy them when they are needed it will not be too painful. Shop around when you do come to make your purchases.

WORK BENCH

It is very important to have a secure, tidy, and solid area from which to work. Try to organise your tool kit in an easy to find manner and save leftover jars and tubs to store a selection of screws, nails, nuts, and bolts. Start practising your skills, and put up some basic shelves to store these items.

Try to keep the bench clear so working is easier by hanging up your tools. The bench needs to be as sturdy as possible so you can mount your vice at one end to help with cutting tasks. Make sure there is plenty of good overhead lighting if you do not have a window. You may want to put up some old sheets as curtains if you feel people may show an interest in the contents of your workshop. Also fit a quality lock and / or padlock to keep it secure.

PREPARATION

The end result of your DIY task will always be determined by the quality of your preparation. There can be a tendency in the early attempts to rush the preparation to get to the end result. However, if you are painting or wall papering, good preparation is everything.

REMOVING WALLPAPER

Removing wallpaper can be a tedious job. Much depends on how it was hung in the first place. You can hire wallpaper strippers, but in most cases this is not necessary. Try to peel off any loose paper using a scraper, making sure not to dig into the plaster work. Score the remaining wallpaper in diagonal lines with the scraper, again not too deep as to damage the wall beneath. Wet the paper with a sponge and a bucket of warm water, and let it soak in. Repeat this 2 or 3 times and try to scrape again. With a few repeat soakings all the paper should come off.

Let the wall dry and brush off any loose dust. Remove any nails or screws that have been used to hang pictures etc. It is always advisable to remove old wall plugs too. To do this screw a large screw into the wall plug with just a few turns of the screwdriver. Then, using pliers, grab the screw and lever out the wall plug. Using ready mixed filler and your scraper, fill any holes and cracks. If the holes are particularly deep fill them in small layers, letting the filler dry before applying the next layer. Work the filler well into all cracks and dents, and leave it slightly proud of the wall.

Following the manufacturer's advice, let the filler dry completely. You will then need to sand the wall down. If you are using an electric sander it will be much quicker, but be prepared for a lot of dust! To sand by hand, use an off cut of timber (2 x 2 x 6" long approx.) and wrap a sheet of sandpaper around it. Go over the wall in a systematic pattern. Use the flat of your hand to feel for any ridges and bumps, and remove them. Wash any remaining dust from the walls with a damp sponge. If the walls are in a kitchen it may also be worth using a sugar soap solution to remove any remaining grease.

If you take short cuts at this stage you will never achieve a quality end result.

PREPARING WOODWORK

Preparing woodwork requires the same detailed approach. If you are painting new wood, check for splits and knot holes, and fill if necessary with wood filler. Undercoat the wood with a 'primer and undercoat'. We would suggest at least two coats to ensure a good final finish. After the second coat is dry, rub it down with a fine grade sandpaper and dust off.

MEASURING

"Measure twice, cut once", is an old but very true saying. When cutting timber it is critical that you accurately take measurements. If there is distance between where you are measuring and where you are cutting, write it down. Never assume that the pre-cut end of your timber is square, so always measure both sides of the piece to be cut.

Mark these measurements with a pencil on either side of the timber, and using a carpenter's square, draw the cut line across the timber. If one end of the timber is going to be visible, make sure when you measure that the pre-cut end is the visible one.

When measuring wallpaper always consider the repeat on the pattern so that it lines up exactly.

DRILLING

Drilling holes is probably one of the first jobs attempted by all budding DIYers. However, there are many who can tell stories about costly and potentially dangerous mistakes.

PUTTING UP SHELVES

If you are putting up a shelf unit, look at the wall plugs supplied and fit the appropriate sized masonry drill bit to your drill. Check the wall with your detector to ensure you are not drilling anywhere near water pipes or electric cables. Measure the depth of the wall plug and mark this on the drill bit with a piece of tape to ensure you drill only to the right depth. Once you have marked where you need the holes, hold the drill level at 90 degrees to the wall and firmly drill into it. Keep checking that you stay level and square, and stop when you have reached the required depth.

Some walls can be particularly hard, and this may require the 'hammer' setting on your drill. With hollow stud walls considerably less effort is needed, but it is essential that you use the correct wall plug to avoid the fixing pulling out.

The same principle is used when drilling into wood; the only difference is that you will use a wood drill bit. When fixing particularly big pieces of timber with large screws it is always advisable to drill a small pilot hole. This not only makes the fixing easier, but also prevents the screw from splitting the timber.

FIXING

Once you have your holes in the walls you must select the right type of wall plug. With solid brick walls the main variance is the size. These are colour coded and will need to be compatible with the size of screw you are using. Tap the appropriate plug into the hole, ensuring it fits tightly. When you are fitting the screw, make sure the wall plug does not start to turn. If it does it will not be secure. Try putting in the next bigger size of plug and screw.

With stud walls there is a huge selection of products on the market. They will all have a weight listing, letting you know if they are light, medium or heavy weight. Follow the manufacturer's instructions to ensure a safe fixing. As with all fixings, do not over tighten them as there may be a possibility of stripping the screw or the fixing in the wall.

When fixing two pieces of timber together we always prefer to use screws rather than nails. Place the 2 pieces of timber together to see if they fit as required. Drill small pilot holes, ensuring they are the right depth and square, and choose the right length and width of wood screw. If in doubt ask your local supplier who will happily help you. Place a small amount of wood glue on one face of the joints and screw them together.

SAWING

To correctly saw a piece of timber you must have a good, sharp saw, and a solid surface on which to do the sawing. The wood should not be too high, but should be made secure by using either a clamp or a vice.

To start the cut, place the saw blade on the marked line and draw back the saw to create a starting point. Repeat this several times to avoid the saw slipping off the marked line. The secret is a 2 way action; cut with

firm pressure on the down stroke and release on the up stroke. As you saw into the wood, increase the angle of the saw to almost 90 degrees. Keep a close eye on the line and make sure you do not deviate from it, and that you keep the saw square and upright. When you come to the end of the cut, support both ends of the timber to avoid it splitting.

PAINTING

Painting is one of the lower risk jobs we can do around the house. Cheap brushes are a waste of time and money as you will spend more time picking hairs off the walls than you will painting them. Always clean your brushes thoroughly after each use, following the instructions on the paint tin. As previously mentioned in the preparation section, planning is the key to success.

Walls

Start by cutting in all edges with a 2" brush. Hold the brush parallel to the seam and with a medium loaded brush, apply to the edge with a smooth, confident stroke. To avoid big mistakes it always pays to practice this technique before implementing it in your final task.

Dependent on the size of the walls to be painted you may choose to use a roller. They are quicker, but be careful as they can flick hundreds of tiny splashes everywhere! Never overload a brush or roller, and avoid putting on

too much paint in one stroke. It will always produce a better finish if you apply 2 good coats rather than trying to save time with one thick coat.

Doors

With your door correctly prepared and undercoated it is time to put on your final finished coat. Remove the door handles and store them safely. This will make painting easier, and will avoid unnecessary mistakes. Put a dust sheet under the door and wedge it open so you can get at all the surfaces. This will also stop the door from moving as you paint.

With a panelled door, paint the mouldings first, then the insides of the panels, making sure you paint in the direction of the wood. Then paint the vertical section followed by the horizontal sections at the top, middle and bottom. Finish by painting the frame and edges of the door. If the door contains glass panels it pays to spend a little time using masking tape

to mask off the glass edges. This will help to prevent any run-overs, and will make painting quicker. Do not remove the tape until the paint is completely dry.

It is highly recommended that you paint each coat in a single process. This will prevent any ridges in the final finish. Only replace the door handles when the paint is fully dry.

In The Garden

There are a vast number of practical jobs to do around the garden, and unfortunately far too many to mention them all here. One of the main ones that we undertake is fencing, whether for privacy, decoration, or crop protection.

PUTTING UP A FENCE

There are many ways in which you can put up a fence. The methods range from post spikes for ground fixing to

metal brackets to fix it to a concrete base.

We are going to look at putting up a fence in the ground, but experience has taught us that to get the best and longest lasting results, using concrete is the most certain way.

The spikes are very convenient, but they are prone to problems. They have a tendency to go in at an angle as you drive them into the ground, and the post can wobble when inserted into them.

Use a piece of string to mark the line of the fence, from the beginning to the end. Cut a piece of battening to the length of the fence panel to help you space the posts.

At the appropriate post mark, dig a hole no less than 50cm (20") deep and 30cm (12") square. Insert the post and pour in a little gravel to keep it in position. Check all the uprights using a spirit level and pour in a readymade quick drying post mix (available from most DIY stores). Firm it in and check the uprights again. Follow the post mix manufacturer's instructions by adding the water and leave it to set. The post will always last longer if it has been treated.

Once you have set all your posts and they have hardened, fix the gravel board (a piece of hard timber to avoid panel rot) level on the bottom of the posts. Make sure it is just above ground level. Secure the panel retaining clips supplied to the posts with screws. Slot the panels in from the top and screw to the clips. Nail a post cap to the top of each post to avoid damp getting into the grain of the posts.

In another chapter we talk about composting and its benefits. Many councils now supply plastic bins at greatly reduced prices, and delivered to your door. However, you may wish to make your own. You could build more than one and collect leaf compost as well as food and gardening waste and grass cuttings. On our website **www.attainableselfsufficiency. co.uk** we have detailed how to build some different designs suitable for all garden sizes.

So the message is make sure you have the right tools for the task, prepare well in advance, and take care and patience to get a great end result.

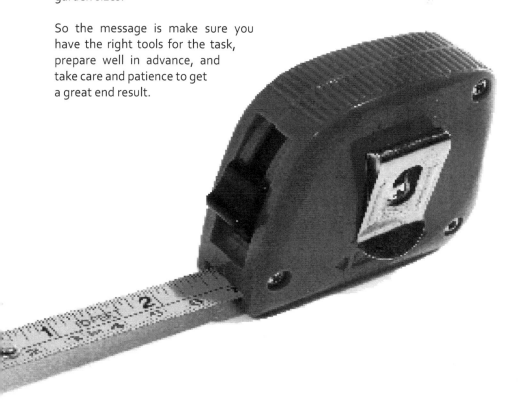

ENERGY EFFICIENCY

The Internet is such a valuable tool. Take a look at the various comparison sites to see if you can get a better deal for gas, electricity and heating fuel. Companies offer better deals if you pay by direct debit and opt for paperless billing.

If you don't have a water meter then it may well be worth doing some research to see if you would benefit by having one fitted.

Simple everyday tips include:

- *Insulating lofts, water tanks, and pipes.*
- *Fill gaps around window frames and skirting boards.*
- *Use energy saving light bulbs, and turn off lights when leaving a room.*
- *Close curtains at dusk. Use draft excluders and heavy curtains around doors. Consider buying thermal blinds or thermal curtains.*

- *Put a jumper on and turn down the thermostat!*
- *Only wash clothes when you have a full load, and dry clothes outside whenever possible.*
- *Get your boiler serviced regularly.*
- *Check seals on fridges and freezers.*
- *Mend dripping taps.*
- *Have a water jug in the fridge for drinking.*
- *Turn the tap off when cleaning your teeth.*

www.energysavingtrust.org.uk gives impartial advice to anyone looking to save energy and reduce carbon emissions. **www.warmfront.co.uk** is a government funded scheme which awards grants for insulation and heating improvements. **www.water-guide.org.uk** offers advice on how to save water in your home and garden.

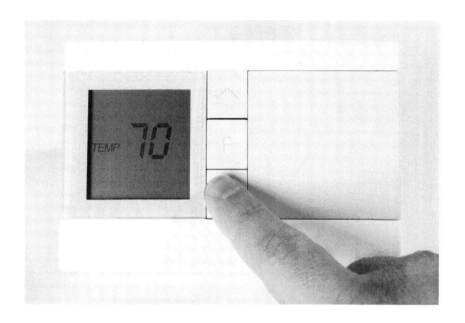

KEEPING THE HEAT IN WITH DIY SECONDARY DOUBLE GLAZING

This may well be worth looking at if you want to stop heat escaping from your windows, but can't afford full double glazing. Secondary double glazing adds a second sheet of glass or perspex to a window frame. There are various options, including having them hinged so you can open the window, but the cheapest option is to simply cover the original window.

Remember though to leave some windows so that you can still get fresh air into the room, and you can get out in case of an emergency. The simplest kit that we have seen is from **www. magnetick.co.uk**. Their kits are held to the original frame with magnetic strips.

A cheap way of sealing the windows for the winter season is to use plastic film. This is available from DIY shops, but if the film gets wet it will begin to peel off the window frames, and you will need to repaint the frames in the summer months, but it's better than nothing at all. For an even cheaper solution use Clingfilm and sticky tape! You will need to use a hairdryer to tighten the film.

Energy saving radiator panels reflect the heat given off the radiator back into the room. Without using these 70% of the heat goes into the wall, and only 30% actually heats your room! They are easy to fit and can save you up to 20% off your heating bills. **www. doctorenergy.co.uk** also has many energy saving products.

FRUIT TO GROW

There's something very special about growing and eating your own fruit. The taste of home-grown fruit is, in our opinion, so much better than shop-bought. If you grow organically you'll also be safe in the knowledge that yours has not been sprayed with pesticides.

Apart from bananas and citrus fruits it has taken us three years to grow enough fruit to feed a family of three. We are able to grow enough to both pick and eat during the growing season, and to preserve for the winter time.

To begin with, make a list of the types of fruit you would like to grow. We also think that it's a good idea to buy both younger and more established plants so that you can begin to enjoy your crops sooner. You will need to decide how much space you have available for fruit, what kind of soil you have, and whether you have a south or north facing garden.

It is far better to grow soft fruits in fruit cages, otherwise you will be fighting the birds for your crops, and you'll probably lose! You can either build your own fruit cages or buy them. The bought ones will probably last longer and look better, but your budget will make the decision for you.

Don't plant your fruit trees in your vegetable plot as they will shade other plants.

In the following section we've written a synopsis for planting and growing some different types of fruit to give you a basic idea of how to go about it.

TREE TYPES

Depending on the size of your plot you may decide that you would like to grow some fruit trees. The standard sized tree is probably going to be too big for most plots, but you can get the following:

BUSH

These have a height and spread of 8-18' (2.6-5.8m). Apples, cherries, plums and pears can all be grown as bush trees.

DWARF PYRAMID

These will have a spread of around 4' (1.2m) and a height of 7' (2.1m.)

CORDON

A cordon has a main trunk and short, fruiting branches. Apples and pears grown this way can be planted 2.5-3' (80cm-1m) apart along a wall, or be supported by wire and posts. They can be planted upright or at a slant. If you only have a small space available, this may be an option for you.

ESPALIER

An espalier is an apple or pear tree planted against a wall or fence. The main trunk is grown vertically, with the branches trained to grow horizontally.

FAN

These are small trees, typically peach, apricot and nectarine, planted against a wall. The main trunk grows vertically, and the branches are grown in a fan shape around the main trunk.

FAMILY TREE

It is possible to find dwarf trees which have either three different varieties of apples or pears grafted onto a single rootstock. The varieties will pollinate each other, giving you a longer fruiting season.

APPLES AND PEARS

The most important thing to consider when thinking about growing apples and pears is to take into acoount how much room you have, and what shape of tree will most suit your needs. Once you have made your decision the best way forward is to consult a specialist grower as there are so many varieties on the market.

SOFT FRUIT

BLUEBERRIES

Blueberries are best grown in pots as they need acidic soil. We use ericaceous compost for ours. Start by using a smaller pot and then re-pot in early spring. They will need to be well watered during the spring and summer. They don't like tap water, so set up a water barrel or two and use rainwater. For best cross pollination, it's best to have three different varieties; if you choose these carefully it is possible to grow blueberries right through the summer and autumn.

RASPBERRIES

Only buy plants that have been certified free of viruses as raspberries can be prone to infections. By looking at different varieties you can grow raspberries all through the summer and autumn. Raspberries will tolerate most soils, but add plenty of organic matter and topsoil before planting. This will help to keep the moisture in. Also don't choose a windy position.

Summer raspberries will need a support system. Put a post at either end of your bed with two wires running horizontally between them, one at 2' (60cm), and one at 5' (1.5m). Autumn varieties don't grow so tall, so won't need supporting.

It is possible to use new canes that grow from your plants, as long as they are disease free. You will need to buy new stock every eight years as the yield begins to deteriorate after this.

STRAWBERRIES

Strawberries are one of the best fruits to try as they are so easy to grow. Again, by researching your varieties it is possible to eat them well into autumn.

Choose a sunny, sheltered spot, and don't grow them where tomatoes or chrysanthemums have grown, as they are all prone to the disease verticillium wilt.

Strawberries will need to be well watered in the spring and summer, and do best with drip irrigation, as watering from overhead can rot the fruit.

You can plant the runners which will grow from the old plants, but you will need to buy new stock every five years or so.

LOGANBERRY

Believed to be a cross between a blackberry and a raspberry, it has dark red berries which are a little bigger than a raspberry. They are quite tart, so will need sugar added to them, but they freeze well and make great pies. Loganberries need sun, don't like winds, and are generally more tender plants than either blackberries or raspberries.

BOYSENBERRY

This is a cross between a blackberry, loganberry and raspberry. When the berries are ready to eat they turn a rich dark purple colour, and the fruits are larger than a blackberry. Boysenberries are hardy and resistant to drought. They like full sunshine, don't like to be in the wind, and make great jam!

GOOSEBERRY

Gooseberries are hardy plants, and can be either sweet or sour. The sweet varieties can be eaten raw, and the sour varieties are used for making jam and wine. They will tolerate some shade and can be grown on a north facing wall, but will need some protection from the wind.

CHERRIES

You can grow both sweet and acid cherry trees. Sweet cherries are for eating fresh, whilst acid Morello cherries are used for jam making, pies, and preserves. It's a good idea to have a look at the newer varieties as they tend to self fertilise, which means you can grow just one tree. Cherry trees can be grown as a full sized tree (15-20'), a fan trained tree on semi-dwarfing stock (12'), or a fan-trained tree on a dwarfing Gisela 5 or Tabel rootstock (8-10'). When buying a cherry tree look for one that is as similar as possible to the shape you're looking for as they don't like hard pruning.

GOJI BERRIES

These are best bought as two year old plants as by this time they are fully hardy. Goji berries are grown as a bush or hedge, and reach full production at four years old. They will tolerate shade but prefer sunshine, and will cope with most soil types. When you harvest your goji berries you must not touch them with bare hands as they will oxidise and turn black. Instead, shake the fruit from the bush.

BLACKCURRANTS

Blackcurrants will tolerate most soil conditions, but will thrive best in well drained, slightly heavy soil. They like to be in the full sun, but will put up with some shade. Avoid any frost pockets. When buying new stock, always buy those that are certified free of viruses. As with all fruit, make sure that they are well watered in the spring and summer. If you are growing them in pots, re-pot them every three years.

RED AND WHITE CURRANTS

Red and white currant bushes are hardy and like sunny positions, but will tolerate some shade. They prefer a well drained, rich soil, but will grow in most soils. They can also be grown on a north facing wall. Avoid frost pockets and windy positions. Both red and white currant bushes produce a large amount of fruit during the mid summer.

GRAPES

It is possible to grow grapes outside in this country, but you will need a warm and sunny sheltered spot in a south facing garden. You can also grow them in unheated greenhouses. You may be best advised to ask a specialist grower who can tell you which varieties would best suit your needs and location.

KIWI

Kiwi bushes can grow very large, so will need pruning, and they don't fruit until the plant is five years old. They need direct sunlight and shelter, ideally on a south or west facing wall. You can now buy self-pollinating plants, but these generally produce less fruit. Otherwise you will need to buy a male and female plant for cross pollination. One of the best things about kiwi fruit is that they are unlikely to be attacked by pest or disease, and you will be able to store the fruit for up to six weeks in a fridge.

PLUM

You can buy plum trees to suit most gardens. Some are self-fertile, others will need two or more trees to cross pollinate. Again, look at the space you have available. You can buy either cooking or eating varieties, and whilst the tree itself is hardy, the flowers can be killed easily by frost, so choose a sheltered site that isn't a frost pocket.

RHUBARB

Rhubarb is actually a herb. It is hardy and grows from crowns, each of which can live up to fifteen years. It will regenerate itself through the crowns, and the plant itself will live quite happily for decades. Rhubarb will do best in a sunny position, but can cope with partial shade. Do not eat rhubarb leaves as they contain oxalic acid which is poisonous.

GARDENING SKILLS

There are many great gardening books available, all of which will tell you the specifics of particular vegetables or fruits and how to grow them, so we will leave this to them. We will concentrate on the practicalities of what to grow, and ways to help you grow.

PLANNING YOUR GARDEN

Now you've taken the decision to 'grow your own,' you will probably need to re-plan your garden, but before you start digging it up, take some time to plan out exactly what you want to do. Make a wish list of all the fruit and vegetable plants you would like to grow. If you're completely new to gardening, then take a look at what food you buy on a regular basis, and see if you can grow some of those.

Salads and tomatoes are perhaps the most obvious, and once you've tasted the difference between home-grown salad and salad bags, you'll be hooked forever. It also makes sense to grow those crops that taste better grown than bought, such as carrots, beans, spinach etc., especially if space is an issue.

Crops like onions, potatoes etc. are probably better bought, at least initially, as they are cheap to buy and take up a lot of space. Rocket is a good salad crop to try as it is incredibly easy to grow and expensive to buy. Look at crops that can be used in a variety of ways. Spinach can be used both raw in salads or cooked.

Once you've made your list, the second and probably biggest consideration will be who uses the garden? If you have children they are going to need some play area. Also, find out which direction your garden is facing, where and when it gets the sun, will you need wind breaks, or is your garden sheltered?

Depending on the size of your plot you will need to think about watering, so consider having water butts either

around the garden or so you can catch the rain water coming from your roof (see Chapter 23).

You want to make your garden as easy to maintain as you can. Being able to walk around your plot and get to everything easily, especially when it's raining, is a must, so plan some paths. You don't have to have raised beds for growing in, but they do make a vegetable garden look nice, and you can easily make them yourself. They can be almost any size, but try not to make them bigger than 6' long or wider than 3'. This way you will be able to reach the middle section (see 'Making a raised vegetable bed').

If you live in an urban area, cats may be a problem; you certainly don't want them using your vegetable plot as a toilet. If you have chickens they will also play havoc with the garden. The idyllic scene of chickens meandering around the veg patch is fiction. They are locusts and will eat anything and everything! You could try having a tall fence around your garden to keep the lazy ones at bay! You could also try having a chicken wire fence around your growing plot. This needs to be at least three feet high. Sonic repellents are also said to work, and cats apparently dislike the smell of lavender and citrus, so you could try sprinkling them around.

Whatever size area you are going to redesign, you may find it useful to sketch some ideas out on paper. You don't have to be an artist, just try to draw out your garden shape. From there you can play with different ideas.

Once you have a plan that you are happy with, invest in some canes and

at least one ball of string. In the past, when we have been redesigning a new patch of land, we have found it really helpful to stake out the design using the canes and string. By doing this you will be able to see how much space you will have for everything, and you will probably find that some things that worked on paper won't work in practice. Just don't do this exercise on a windy day, or if you're trying to look after children, granny, or the dog.

HOW TO MAXIMISE YOUR SPACE

THE SMALL GARDEN

If you don't have a lot of space but would still like to grow your own, you can. When you are buying your seeds, look out for ones that are dwarf varieties. These vegetable plants have been bred so that the plant itself is small so you can fit them into a small area. It is also possible to buy 'patio' fruit trees.

You can try planting vegetables with your flowers. This may make them a little more difficult to harvest, but it can be done. Crops that grow upwards like beans or other vine varieties such as cucumber can produce tremendous crops.

Succession planting is a method by which you plant a small amount of seeds of different varieties every two weeks to get continual cropping throughout the season. The amount of seeds you plant should be dependent on your own needs.

A lot of herbs and vegetables can be grown in pots. All you need are the seeds and compost, then just water

as needed – easy! Growing in pots has the advantage that it's very clean, but you will need to keep your plants well watered, especially in hot weather as compost tends to dry out quickly. If you add one part vermiculite to three parts compost, this should help with water retention.

You can use almost any kind of pot to plant in, but whatever you use it will need to have drainage holes in the bottom, and it is a good idea to choose a light colour pot as dark colours will absorb more heat which could be a problem during a hot summer. You can also just plant straight into grow bags, or do as we do and plant potatoes in old builders' bags.

Pre-made raised vegetable kits can also play their part. These kits are available in different sizes and made of rigid plastic which you simply slot together and fill with soil and compost. At the end of the season they can be packed away if needed. There are many on the market, ranging from economical to very expensive.

If you live in a flat and only have a balcony, don't despair! It's possible to buy four-tier growing houses into which you can slot your growing pots. Using these it will still be possible to grow salads, carrots, beans, and spinach, to name but a few.

THE LARGER GARDEN

If you have more land then you will obviously have more freedom to grow fruit and vegetables, and perhaps

keep chickens. We have about a third of an acre, and over the years we have divided it up into different sections. We now have a rose garden, a pond area, two fruiteries, and a large rabbit-proofed vegetable garden, plus a section in which we grow and sell flowers.

Each area has been redesigned individually, and this has been done gradually over time. We have always begun the process by doing some sketches, maybe also taking some photographs, and then planning out the area with string and canes.

As we are in a rural position, each new area needs rabbit-proofing, and we have found that unless you grow fruit inside some sort of cage, the birds will eat the lot! From a personal point of view we also think it's important to have an area where you can just sit and relax as well as having the productive parts of your garden, so perhaps plan for a space to think in.

KNOWING YOUR SOIL

Soil is divided into six categories; clay, loamy, peaty, chalky, silty, and sandy. Knowing what type of soil you have will help you know what you can plant, and how to work the soil to your advantage. Most soil is a mixture of the following, but whatever soil you have you will always need to look after it and add plenty of manure, both green and animal, to keep up the nutritional values.

Clay soil tends to be very heavy and clumpy, and becomes easily

waterlogged, but it has a high nutrient level. You will need to loosen it with sand or compost.

Loamy soil is made up of 40% silt, 40% sand, and 20% clay. It is rich in nutrients and keeps its moisture without becoming waterlogged.

Peaty soil is more acidic than other types, and therefore contains more organic matter as the matter takes longer to rot. It also has fewer nutrients and can become waterlogged.

Chalky soil is alkaline and contains a lot of stones. It will also dry out quickly in the summer. You will need to add a lot of soil improvers such as fertiliser, manure etc.

Silty soil is excellent as it contains a lot of nutrients, is easy to work with, and has good moisture retention.

Sandy soil needs organic matter adding to it to help water retention and keep nutrient levels up. It does warm up early in the season, so is good for early crops.

PH LEVELS

You can buy inexpensive soil pH testing kits from most garden centres, and it's worth doing this as you will then know if your soil is acid or alkaline. From pH6 to 7 is neutral and best as most plants will thrive. 5 to 6 is fairly acid, but good for tomatoes, potatoes and fruit. Above pH7 is alkaline and will need compost and manure adding to the soil. Spinach, brassicas, plums, apples and peaches all like this type of soil.

Whatever soil you have you will need to feed it in order to keep it healthy, high in nutrients, and to aid water retention. Each year add plenty of compost, manure, and other organic matter.

EASING THE WORKLOAD

Living a more self-sufficient lifestyle will make you fitter and keep you busy, but you'll also want to balance this with making things as easy to manage as possible. One tip that we have found invaluable is the use of heavy duty weed control membrane. We use this both for the paths and for planting through as it really does cut down on the amount of weeding you have to do. The membrane itself is black and comes on a roll. You simply clear the area you are working on, pin it to the ground with plastic pegs, then we add bark on top for weight.

For our fruit and flowers we then simply cut a hole in the membrane and plant. This has saved us so much time weeding. We just wish we had used this system years ago. You do still get some weeds coming through, but you'll find that they are weak and easy to remove.

The bark on top not only adds weight, but also acts as a mulch to keep the moisture in. You will need to add more bark every two years or so, but

don't buy it from a garden centre as it will cost you a fortune. Find a local tree surgeon who can deliver a load to you.

WHAT TO GROW

If your long term goal is to become more self-sufficient and rely less on buying in your groceries, you will need to have a good idea about the quantity and type of fruit and vegetables that you buy on a regular basis. The best way of doing this is to create a spreadsheet and list all those fruits and vegetables that you buy over a four month period. At the end of this time you should be able to work out what you'll need to grow to feed your family over the year.

Remember that you will need to grow enough to store for the winter months, otherwise you'll end up living on turnips and other root vegetables for the early part of each year, which may cause your family to riot!

The following list of vegetables and fruit is intended as a guide only, as your eating preferences will be the major factor in deciding what you grow, but it will give you some idea of what you would need to plant to feed a family of four with a varied diet. When buying your seeds look at the possibility of having two or more varieties that you can sow early and late into the season.

VEGETABLE	NO. OF PLANTS	VEGETABLE	NO. OF PLANTS
Asparagus	8-15	Beans	10-15
Broccoli	5-7	Sprouts	2-5
Cabbage	4-6	Carrots	Continous sowings
Cauliflower	3-6	Celery	2-8
Corn	15-20	Cucumber	1-2
Leeks	10-20	Lettuce	Continous Sowings
Melon	1-3	Onions	100+
Peas	5-10	Peppers	3-5
Squash	1-3	Tomatoes	1-3
Courgettes	1-3	Chillies	1-3
Parsnips	10-15	Garlic	35+
Spinach	Continuous sowing of the 'perpetual' variety		

SOFT FRUITS

This list is basically what we grow. We are a family of three and are now completely self-sufficient in fruit, except for bananas and citrus fruits. By choosing different varieties we can eat fresh fruit from early summer to late autumn, and have enough to freeze to keep us going over the winter months.

Blueberries	x 7 bushes
Strawberries	30' x 3' patch
Raspberries (summer canes)	x 10
Raspberries, (autumn canes)	x 10
Gooseberry	x 1 bush
Blackcurrant	x 1 bush
Boysenberry	x 1 bush

COMPOST AND MANURE

Making your own compost is not only easy, it is also very cost effective. You are not paying any extra for the ingredients, yet you end up with a product that helps feed and replenish your garden soil. If you have never made your own before do not be put off as it is a straight forward process.

Many Councils supply compost bins of varying sizes either free or at greatly reduced prices. To check if your Council is taking part, go to **www.recyclenow.com** or **www. getcomposting.com** and enter your postcode; you should be able to buy a large bin for less than £10.

You can make your own too, and there are many websites that will give you plans, but to start with a plastic compost bin will be ample.

MANURE

If you are fortunate enough to have stables nearby, go and ask them if they are giving away manure. Most stables are only too happy to get rid of it as an average sized horse will produce over 11,000lb of manure a year!

You can put this on to your vegetable beds, but do not use freshly produced manure as it will be too strong for young plants. One year old manure is much better. We add the horse manure to a compost bin. The reason for this is because most horses are now stabled on sawdust or wood chips, not straw, and this is not crop friendly because as the wood chip breaks down it causes a nitrogen deficiency in the soil. If the horses are bedded on straw this problem does not occur.

GREEN MANURE

Green manures are just as important as animal manures, but less well known or used. Many growers will leave their beds empty between crops and over winter, but by planting green manures valuable nitrogen will be replaced.

Green manures are a range of plants that you can grow, dig in, and let rot to feed the soil. Different varieties can be used for different times of year, and will require different growing times before you dig them in. You can buy the seeds from garden centres, and they are sown directly onto beds.

Not only do they add nitrogen, but they also give good ground coverage, which will suppress weeds. They also improve water retention and develop soil texture.

The 2 types of ingredients that make good compost	
Greens (nitrogen rich)	Brown (carbon rich)
Kitchen waste, nettles, grass cuttings, soft green prunings, and horse manure	Paper, light cardboard, hedge trimmings, sawdust and wood shavings, and old bedding plants

Things not to compost:

- **Meat and fish**
- **Cooked food**
- **Coal or fire ash**
- **Disposable nappies**
- **Pet poo**
- **Weeds with seeds or perennials**

To create a good, balanced compost you need a good mixture of both green and brown. We also introduce a small amount of grass cuttings and fallen leaves.

We shred all our waste paper, and this helps it rot down when added to the compost. It is important to keep the heap turned with a garden fork and moist. You can add compost starters at the beginning of spring to give it a kick start, and you can get these from garden centres.

Site your bin on soil, but beware that rats and foxes may dig under to get in. We discovered rats were frequently entering the bin for dinner, so we wrapped the bottom of the plastic bin with two layers of chicken wire and secured it firmly to the sides. This allows the worms to get in, but keeps unwanted animals out.

Try to leave the compost for as long as possible to give it every chance to rot down. We have 3 bins going at once to ensure a constant supply. We have also built a wire caged bin to keep all the leaves in to make great mulch for the garden.

When the compost is well rotted and looks similar to fine soil, cover your vegetable beds with it in late autumn, and then cover them with a sheet of black plastic. Secure this down for the winter period, and by early spring the worms will have done all the hard work for you, and you'll be ready to plant.

PROPAGATING, SOWING, AND PLANTING ON

For us the real joy of gardening is seeing the whole process from beginning to end; where from a tiny seed you can nurture an array of great, tasty, full grown vegetables. Every different vegetable or herb will have its own particular sowing requirements, which will be listed on its own packet. When you first start growing your own it is advisable to follow these recommendations. As your experience grows you will find your own tricks to help you get the most from your seeds.

It is a very good idea to keep a diary of what, how many, when, and the temperature conditions when you sowed your seeds. This will be of invaluable help when it comes to maximising your crops next year.

43

PROPAGATING

As a rule of thumb most seeds germinate at around 18 to 20 degrees Celsius. To get an early start we use heated propagators which come in a huge range of sizes and types. Seedlings can take from 1 to 3 weeks to germinate, depending on the variety.

Seed propagators are purpose built, pre-wired trays with lids. You simply add a layer of sharp sand and place your pots / seed trays on the sand and cover them. You cannot adjust the temperature, and they can cost up to £40 for a two tray size.

You can use heat mats with a basic un-heated propagator or seed tray. Again you cannot adjust the temperature,

but they are economical.

We use a large five tray holder with a lid and soil warming cables connected to a thermostat. This gives us total control of the temperature, and a large area for propagating seeds in both pots and trays.

Seed propagation is not the only means by which you can grow new plants. There are many others including cuttings, layering, division, and grafting. As we are looking at vegetables and herbs these methods are not relevant, but as your experience and confidence increases you can research further ways to grow yet more plants.

SOWING

Whether sowing directly into the soil where the plant will grow or into trays or pots, it is important to get the conditions right.

When sowing in trays and pots, use seedling compost. This will be finer than your own compost, and will provide the correct water retention. You will notice on some seed packets that it states sow in trays or pots. This, in our opinion, should be down to how much space you have. Wherever possible we try to grow ours in pots, which means less root disturbance. However, parsnips, beetroot, spring onions, and spinach should be sown straight into the ground. The soil must be well dug and as fine as possible.

Most pea seed packets will tell you to sow straight into the ground, but we have found this to be wrong. As soon as they start to shoot the mice and birds eat the tops, and we end up with no crop! Sow in pots with a fine six inch stick to support the initial growth before planting out.

When sowing outside, make sure you mark the rows with short canes, and note on your garden design what you have sown, and where. If you cover the soil with black plastic a couple of weeks prior to sowing out, the soil will be warmer and this will aid germination.

Sowing indoors gives plants a good early start, especially if using a heated propagator. Doing so in individual

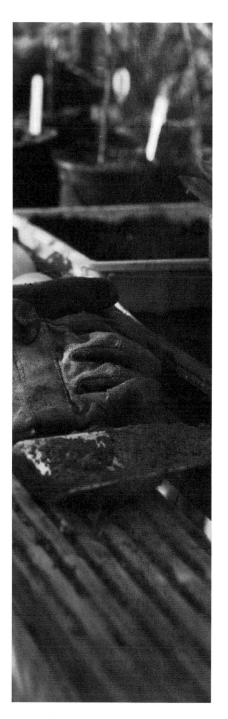

pots makes it easier to give individual seed types the right conditions, and if some germinate earlier than others then they can be moved out of the heated propagator separately.

Do not forget to label your pots. You will be surprised how they all look similar during the early stages of growth, and how quickly you will forget.

PLANTING ON

If you have sown early and all things have gone well, you may be tempted to try and get your seedlings into the ground. Beware any likelihood of frost as it will kill any new seedlings.

Most vegetables plants should have 2 sets of leaves before planting out, but follow the instructions on the seed packet. You can try to cover the soil before planting out to keep it warmer, and using cloches over tender new plants to protect them from any frost. You can either buy these from a garden centre or improvise with clear plastic bottles; you can also cover plants with a fleece tunnel.

Pay special attention when planting out brassicas as they need to be very firmly planted to prevent them from falling over.

As we mentioned at the beginning of this chapter, we are not going into every detail about growing every single vegetable. However, make sure that you keep your growing crops weed free, well fed and watered, and read up on additional advice to ensure you get the maximum yield from your sowings.

PROTECTING YOUR CROPS

There's nothing worse in the garden than seeing all your hard work and investment in time and money being devoured by a selection of unwanted animals and insects.

VEGETABLES

It is important to know who else is also interested in your crop. Our vegetable patch consists of raised beds enclosed in chicken wire fencing to protect against rabbit incursions.

To make it completely rabbit-proof, dig a trench one foot deep and one foot wide around the perimeter of the patch. In each corner sink a 5ft long 3 x 3 inch treated timber post in the inside of each corner. Cutting the end at a steep angle will help you to drive it into the ground. This will involve digging a hole a foot deep in each corner of the trench, leaving three feet of the post above ground. To make sure that the post is secure, and to avoid excess rotting, we secure it in place with rapid setting post cement. Make sure the posts are all upright and square.

Decide where you want your access gate. Again, drive the same sized timbers into the trench to make the hinge and stop posts for your gate. It is important that these are square and

upright, otherwise the gate will not fit, and will let the bunnies in.

You can make your own gate from any size planking, strengthened with cross members. Use large hinges and a robust catch. Remember, it does not have to be a thing of great beauty with lavish new timber, but rather a thing of practicality and value.

We use small gauge chicken wire that is four foot wide. Measure the distance between your posts and cut a length of wire, allowing some spare. Lay the length in the trench so it goes down the front face across the bottom, and up two feet against the posts. Cut a second length and lay it against the back face of the trench. This will be one foot in the trench, and will come up three feet against your

posts. The reasoning behind this is that it gives a double thickness of wire for the first foot that is above ground. Fix one end securely to the post using wire tacks, pull tightly, and secure it to the post at the other end. To help it stay rigid you can use coated metal poles (available from any garden centre) woven through the fencing at 4 to 5 foot intervals, and pushed firmly into the ground. Before you fill in the trench you can put in some weed barrier membrane too. This will help prevent grass growing through the wire, which can be difficult to stop if it gets established.

Once you have filled in the trench, put some membrane across it and cover with bark; this helps to stop weeds and grass growing through your fence. This can seem like a lot

of work, but if done correctly it will last for many years to safeguard your valuable vegetable crops.

If you grow brassicas you may want to net them to stop butterflies and birds damaging your crop. You can buy this from all garden centres, but make sure if you are relying on insects for pollination that you remove the netting at some stage. We find that by encouraging birds into the garden throughout the year that they help remove the caterpillars and slugs the natural way. If they peck a few holes in your cabbage leaves then we think this is a small price to pay for natural gardening.

In addition to this you can use many methods to stop slugs (see Chapter 22).

Carrot fly are the only other thing that eats our veg, and we get around this by planting them in large, tall containers. This not only raises the crop above low flying flies, but also helps produce a good growing medium as opposed to our heavy clay soil.

SOFT FRUIT

The main predators of your soft fruit will be birds. In the earlier stages of our fruit growing we lost a great deal of cherries and gooseberries; they seemed to know the very day the fruit was at its best.

The only real way to stop birds is by having a fruit cage. This is another cash investment, but do go for the best you can afford. The cheaper varieties will not be as strong, and will not last as long. Measure the area you have to put up a fruit cage, and try to get the biggest that you can afford and fit in. Follow the manufacturer's fitting instructions carefully, and we suggest that you use extra camping hooks to secure the netting to the ground all the way around. (The blackbirds around here have learnt to go under the netting!)

Our cherries were completely eaten one year by ants. Tree grease is a non-chemical way of stopping them marching up your trees and devouring your crop. It can be applied either by brush or as strips. Beware as it is very messy. You will need to net your cherry trees, if possible, when the cherries are starting to ripen in order to stop the birds.

MAKING A RAISED VEGETABLE BED

Raised beds improve drainage, allow better access, and easier crop rotation. They are more economical for watering too, have less soil compaction, and you get more crops per square foot. So what's not to like?

You can buy a huge variety of shapes and sizes of raised beds from garden suppliers, but they can cost a fortune. It's not just a cost advantage to build your own though, as you can make the size that best suits your garden.

We have used 6 inch x 1 inch treated planks for the sides, and lengths of 1½ inch treated timber for the fixing posts. Cut the lengths and sides to your required size.

Cut the fixing posts to 10 inch lengths, with a 45 degree cut. Make sure you treat the cut ends

Lay out the planks on a large, flat area in the shape of your bed. Place the fixing post under the side plank flush to the end and drill 2 small holes through the plank and into the post. This will stop the plank from splitting and will make fixing the screws easier. Use 2 inch brass screws and fix the post to the bedside. Repeat this for the other side plank.

Face the end planks up to the 2 side planks and fit the same way.

Once the bed is made, place it where

you want it. Use an offcut of wood to put over the posts and hit them in sequence until they are buried in the ground. Make sure you do this evenly so the bed is level and sits firmly in place.

These will last you for many years, and should work out at a fraction of the cost of bought ones. If you have a local builder's yard they may have offcuts of timber that you can use that will make them even cheaper.

BUILDING A POND

Experts will tell you that when you build a pond it has to be either a fish pond or a wildlife pond, and that you can't mix the two. We totally disagree; our pond is home to a dozen various goldfish, frogs, toads, water boatmen, dragonflies, snails, and even a pair of grass snakes.

OK, so it is not a crystal clear award winning ornamental pond, but the fish have all grown to a ripe old age and are very healthy. They live with the frogs and toads, and they do eat some of the frog spawn each year, but enough survives to ensure the frogs live on.

When planning your pond you must first consider safety. If you have young children, make sure the area is well fenced off. If you are going to fit a filtration system, then make sure a qualified electrician fits the correct armoured cable to supply the power.

Try not to site the pond under trees as autumn will bring a headache with the falling leaves. A quiet, partially shaded area is preferable. When planning, be realistic about the size of pond you want. The wildlife it will attract will be beneficial to your garden, but you don't want to turn it into water world!

You can buy pre-formed plastic ponds, but they are expensive and do not give you scope to build what you might want. Make sure when you are digging the hole that you have one end of the pond that slopes to the edges like a beach. This will help frogs get out and birds bath and drink. The deep end should be at least 2 foot deep to help your fish survive in winter. Try to have ledges and varying depths to encourage different wildlife. Once you have dug the hole to the required shape and depth, check it thoroughly for any sharp stones and remove them. Cover the pond bottom and sides with an inch thick layer of builder's sand to ensure that the pond liner does not tear.

There are varying qualities of pond liner. Basic PVC liner is cheap, but will become brittle over the years, and cannot be repaired. Butyl rubber pond liner is very flexible, lasts considerably longer, and can be repaired, but it will cost more. As always, buy the best you can afford. Most websites that sell pond liners will have a page to help you calculate the amount of liner you need.

Lay the liner in the pond and try to

remove any creases and wrinkles. Do not be tempted to trim the edges at this stage. If like us you are going to fit a filtration system, make sure that you have read the instructions of the system to ensure that your design will be satisfactory for your pump. Talk to a professional at your local garden centre as to which pump will best fit your pond and your budget.

If you can use rain or well water to fill your pond it will be much better. If you are using tap water you should let it stand for at least twenty four hours to help any chlorine evaporate, but you may need to treat the water to eliminate chloramines, which will not evaporate. Always follow the instructions on any packet of water treatment with great care.

Once the pond is full you will need to trim and cover the edges of the liner. We have used ornamental flat stones to keep the edges covered. At the shallow end introduce a selection of round, smooth stones across the width of the pond. This gives a place for the frogs and toads to spawn where the fish can't get at them. If you have a friend who has a pond with a good selection of wildlife in it, ask if you can have an amount of water from it. Use cleaned, plastic water bottles to bring the water to your pond. It will help the wildlife establish itself a little quicker.

It will also help if you have some plant life in your pond; speak to your garden centre for advice. There are also many websites that will help you choose the appropriate plants for your size pond.

Once you are sure the conditions are satisfactory you can introduce your fish. To make sure that your fish do not become an easy lunch for a heron it is essential that you fit pond netting. Leave a foot or so free at the shallow end so the birds can bath and drink though. On several occasions we have had to cut the grass snakes free from the netting, as they try to slide through it to get to the water. If you have grass snakes, try to raise the netting a couple of inches off the ground all around the pond.

HOUSEHOLD HINTS

Use cereal bags to store frozen food.

Use your oven twice when it is on.

Use rechargeable batteries with a solar powered battery charger.

Don't use air fresheners - open a window.

Don't buy bottled water – use a filter. Alternatively, nobody has yet died from tap water in the UK.

To remove a stubbon wall plug from the wall, screw in a large screw, turn it a couple of times, and pull it out with a pair of pliers.

A little soap on a screw stops it getting stuck in wood.

To loosen stubbon screws, place a screwdriver on the head of the screw and tap the end with a hammer. Spray a little WD40 or vinegar onto the screw to help loosen it.

A saw will cut more smoothly with some soap on the cutting edge.

Drill pilot holes when fixing large screws or nails to avoid splitting the wood.

To avoid dust when drilling into a wall, ask a friend to hold the nozzle of the vacuum cleaner by the drill, or use a piece of paper stuck to the wall with masking tape beneath the drill.

Remove wax from clothes by a cool iron through 2 sheets of brown paper.

Stop your salt going damp by ading 3 or 4 grains of uncooked rice to it.

Always wipe greasy pans with kitchen paper before washing up to save blocking your drains.

Wear washing up gloves to remove stubborn jar lids.

Bicarbonate of soda, lemon juice and cream of tartar remove tea and coffee stains from cups.

Never throw away vegetable water. It's a good base for soups, and full of vitamins.

If an egg floats in water, throw it away.

Draw a chalk line on the floor to stop ants. They will not cross it.

Use candle wax or soap to make wooden drawers run smoothly.

Before you make a large purchase, always get 3 separate quotes.

If you don't have a dual flush toilet, partially fill a balloon with water and place it in your cistern to reduce water usage.

Think twice before nipping out in the car.

Keep a pad and pencil in the kitchen to note what you need from the shops.

Use free directory enquiries (0800 100 100) rather than more expensive ones ,or use the Internet.

Avoid 0870 numbers. Check out **www. saynoto0870.co.uk** for alternatives.

INSECTS

For anyone who grows organically, turning the garden into a paradise for beneficial insects can pay great dividends. It's really worthwhile trying to attract ladybirds, lacewings, and hoverflies etc., as they will eat problem bugs and save you time and money in the process.

The secret to creating a wildlife haven is to try and recreate as best you can the habitats found in nature. When you look at your garden, try to incorporate aspects of water, meadow, hedgerow, woodland, and wetland, plus a patch left to go 'wild'.

Building a pond is probably one of the most useful things you can do to attract wildlife (see Chapter 7). A garden pond will attract a host of insects such as dragonflies, damselflies, water spiders and water boatmen. It will also be a good breeding ground for midges, which in turn are a good food source for birds.

If you don't have room for even a small pond, think about placing 'watering bowls' in various places around your garden. Make sure that each one contains stones to prevent birds and insects falling in and drowning.

Sowing and growing wild flowers in your garden is a lovely way of attracting beneficial insects and birds. Flower colours and scent play an important part in pollination; the colours acts like flags, attracting insects to their flowers. For instance, butterflies like yellows and blues, bees like blues, reds, and purples, and moths go for white. Butterflies like heavy scents and bees prefer lighter, sweeter ones.

Leave the heads on flowers such as sunflowers, teasel and echinacea so that the birds can feed on their seeds in winter.

Hedgerows provide shelter for both birds and insects. If you're planting afresh, think about growing three to five different hedge varieties such as hawthorn, dog rose, hazel, and evergreens. This way the hedge will provide berries and shelter both in the summer and winter months.

If you have the room, a woodland area would, over time, attract insects to inhabit the leaf mould. Insects need dark, damp, and undisturbed habitats to flourish, so even if you don't have room for a woodland area, try to have a few sections in your garden where you can have piles of logs, branches, stones etc.

Leave a small patch of nettles growing in the full sun. Nettles attract the nettle aphid, which is good news as they only feed on nettles, but will be food for ladybirds and hoverflies, and will support butterflies and moths.

You can also give your insects a helping hand by buying or making special 'insect habitats' to attract them to your garden.

THE GOOD GUYS!

APHIDIUS

These are small, black parasitic wasps about 2mm long. The females lay single eggs into young greenfly or blackfly, which then swell and appear mummified. Once the egg hatches, the larvae of the aphidius develops inside the aphid and eventually kills it. Aphidius are best introduced as soon as the first aphid is spotted as they work better on small patches of aphids. They are only for use in greenhouses or conservatories.

LADYBIRDS

There are forty varieties of ladybird in this country, and each one can eat up to fifty aphids per day. They hibernate in winter, and wake up in April. You can help them by having a horizontal pile of hollow dead stems placed in a dry, sheltered spot such as the bottom of a hedge.

HOVERFLIES

These look like wasps, but are harmless. The adults love nectar and pollen, but in their larval stage they will eat aphids such as greenfly and thrups. After feeding the females will lay their eggs on colonies of aphids, so that the larvae can feed off them when they hatch.

LACEWINGS

Both the adults and larvae will eat aphids. The larvae will eat around 200 aphids before becoming adults. They like cool, dry shelters such as garden sheds and barns.

DRAGONFLIES

These beautiful creatures are carnivorous and mainly eat mosquitoes and midges, but they will feed on other small insects. They lay their eggs in water, so build a garden pond.

GROUND BEETLES

These are black and hunt mainly at night. Their diet is varied and they will eat aphids, caterpillars, leatherjackets, snails, and slugs. They like a damp pile of logs to shelter under.

BROWN CENTIPEDES

These have between thirty and eighty legs and are light brown. They are totally carnivorous and inject their prey with venom. They eat vine weevils and slugs.

NEMATODES

These are long, microscopic parasitic roundworms that live in soil. They use soil living insects and larvae in their reproductive cycle. This will kill the insect host within twenty four to forty eight hours. Weevils, beetles, flies, ants, fleas, snails, and grubs can all be killed using nematodes.

To use nematodes you will need to know the exact problem you have in your garden so you can order the correct nematode species.

Follow the manufacturer's advice on how to apply the nematodes, but this usually means mixing them with non-chlorinated water and spraying the soil using either a hand spray or watering can. As nematodes attack the larval stage of their hosts they will only kill the next generation of pests, but they are a useful tool for organic gardeners.

BUTTERFLIES

Apart from their beauty, butterflies are plant pollinators, second only to bees in terms of importance.

THE BAD GUYS!

APHIDS

Aphids are very common sap sucking insect pests which cause a plant's leaves to curl as well as causing stunted growth. They are also known as greenfly or blackfly, but they can be yellow, pink, mottled, or white. Aphids excrete a sticky substance which enables black soot mould to grow, and they also transmit viruses which can be a problem for strawberries, raspberries and tomatoes.

Aphids are eaten by ladybirds, hoverflies and lacewing larvae, and some parasitic wasps. Companion planting can also help, so if you plant tagetes, calendula, poached egg plant, and morning glory near your crops, these will attract the ladybirds etc., which will feed on the aphids. You can also rub them off with your fingers or spray diluted washing up liquid on affected plants. Use one teaspoon of washing up liquid to two litres of water. Aphids breathe through their skin, so this will suffocate them.

CABBAGE WHITE CATERPILLARS

These will devour your brassicas if you're not careful. One of the best ways to stop this is to cover your plants with very fine netting. The netting has to be fine, otherwise the adult butterflies will be able to get through the net and lay their eggs.

Flowers that attract beneficial insects			
Winter aconite	Provides early pollen for insects and bees	Buddleia	Butterflies and bees
Chamomile and daisy	Hoverflies and wasps	Poached egg plant	Hoverflies and bees
Comfrey, common or field	Bees and butterflies	Poppy	Hoverflies and bees
Cowslip	Provides early nectar for insects	Flowering currant	One of the best sources of spring nectar for bees
Foxgloves	Bumble bees	Honeysuckle	Bumble bees, but also blackfly which in turn attract lacewings and ladybirds
Hyssop	Lacewings and bees	Lupins and sunflowers	Aphidius
Pot marigold	Hoverflies and wasps	Rosemary	Bees, butterflies, and hoverflies
Wild garlic	Butterflies, wasps, and flying insects		

JUICING

The key benefit of juicing is to give our bodies the right vitamins, minerals, nutrients, and antioxidants to boost and prolong healthy well-being. Some of the many benefits of juicing include:

- Greatly helping and supporting a weight-loss programme
- Speeding up recovery from illness
- Promoting healthier, younger looking skin

In comparison with cooked vegetables, juiced vegetables and fruits do not lose the levels of those valuable nutrients and vitamins as you use only the raw ingredients. Not many of us would sit down and eat half a pineapple, a banana, and an apple, but juicing makes eating fruit and vegetables more exciting, and could help children increase their intake.

Throughout the day there are different styles of juices that can help you with a list of common conditions brought on by modern living.

WHAT TO JUICE - FRUITS

Apples	Good for the digestive system, immunity and an antioxidant
Apricots	Good for immunity, healthy skin, hair, teeth and bones
Bananas	An energy booster, preserves nerves and skin
Blackberry	Antioxidant, boosts the immune system, anti-ageing properties
Blackcurrant	Antioxidant, boosts immune system, fights degenerative diseases
Cherries	Aids digestion, the immune system, and a powerful antioxidant
Cranberries	Good for urinary infections
Grapes	Can lower blood pressure, help with urinary infections

Grapefruit	Beneficial for stomach and colon cancers, improves circulation
Lemons	Good for treating colds and flu
Limes	Beneficial for good circulation and the nervous system
Mango	Boosts the immune system, controls blood pressure
Meloon	Energy booster and helps preserve the nervous system
Oranges	Anti-cancer properties, fighting colds
Peaches	Helps fight degenerative diseases, reduces blood pressure
Pears	Good for diabetes
Pineapples	Good for the digestive system, can treat blood clots
Prunes	Relieve constipation and great for de-toxing
Raspberries	Can help with weight loss and menstrual irregularities
Strawberries	A good system cleanser and a great antioxidant

WHAT TO JUICE - VEGETABLES

Avocado	Hunger suppressant, boosts immune system, healthy skin and hair
Beetroot	Very good for pregnancy, preserves the nervous system
Broccoli	Good levels of iron and potassium which can help fight cancers
Cabbage	Cell regeneration, can help fight stomach ulcers and heart disease
Carrot	Great antioxidant, helps the digestive system
Celery	Can help arthritis, helps maintain correct fluid levels in the body
Cucumber	Boosts healthy skin, good for hair growth
Garlic	Great antiviral properties, helps against infections
Lees	Aids de-toxing and aids healthy bone growth
Lettuce	Great antioxidant, can help with cancer, promotes a healthy colon
Mangetout	Helps brain functions, stimulates body regeneration
Onions	Good for healthy blood circulation, can fight cholestrerol
Parsley	Helps against anaemia, good for skin structure
Parsnips	Help the appearance of skin and hair, liver cleansing properties
Peppers	Great source of vitamin C, good for treating colds and flu
Spinach	Very good for osteoporosis and great for de-toxing
Tomato	Good protector of muscles, joints and brain cells, good antioxidant
Watercress	Promotes healthy skin and hair, can be good for lung cancer
Wheatgrass	An acquired taste, but an excellent cleanser

RECIPES

There is no hard and fast rule about what goes with what, but if you want some inspiration to start you off we have listed a few of our favourites below. You can make up your own recipes by experimenting with your favourite ingredients, but as a rule try to drink your juice as soon as you can after juicing. This helps you maximise the benefits.

WAKEY WAKEY	
30 grapes 5cm fresh ginger 1 lemon	1 orange 1 pear 1 apple 1 grapefruit
Add the washed grapes, peeled ginger, and chopped peeled lemon to your juicer. Juice and add a little water to achieve your preferred consistency.	Add the peeled and segmented orange and grapefruit to the juicer. Add the roughly chopped, unpeeled apple and pear, and juice.

PICK-ME-UP	
2 carrots ½ cucumber 2 stalks of celery ½ beetroot	200g carrot 100g strawberries 100g beetroot ½ orange
Wash and top and tail the carrot, celery and beetroot. Starting with the beetroot, then the carrot, celery, and finally the cucumber, juice all the ingredients.	Wash and top and tail the carrot and beetroot and juice them along with the peeled orange. Blend the juice with the strawberries and ice, if you require.

DE-STRESS	
2 broccoli florets ½ red pepper 1 carrot 2 sticks of celery A small bunch of parsley 1 large tomato	80g blackcurrants 1 grapefruit 1 apple
Wash and top and tail the carrot and celery. Cut the tomato in half, do the same with the pepper, and remove the stalk. Juice all the ingredients in the order stated above	Peel and roughly chop the grapefruit and chop up the whole apple. Juice in the order stated above

ENERGY BOOSTER	
A large bunch of watercress 2 carrots ½ cucumber	150g spinach 2 apples 1 yellow pepper A pinch of powdered cinnamon
Top and tail the carrot, wash the watercress, and juice in the order stated above.	Quarter the pepper and the apple; wash the spinach, and juice in the order above. Add the cinnamon (optional) at the end.

NIGHT NIGHT	
2 carrots 2 sticks celery 1 small lettuce	100g pineapple 100g grapes ½ small lettuce 2 sticks celery
Top and tail the carrot and the celery. Wash the lettuce and dry in a salad spinner. Juice in the order stated above.	Peel the pineapple and top and tail the celery and juice in the order stated above.

KITCHEN CRAFT

The kitchen is the heart of any house; that's something we all say, but do we truly mean it? In the fast pace of modern living we tend to gloss over the real importance of this crucial space. We tend to miss the great sense of satisfaction and well-being that can be achieved there.

We appreciate that not everybody wants to spend hours each day in the kitchen, but to not give it the importance it deserves is a true shame. To enjoy life we need our health, and for our bodies to be healthy it is essential that we give them the right ingredients. It is not our intention to turn you into award winning chefs, but to share with you our knowledge and love of cooking.

Regardless of the size of your kitchen, it can become the centre of your home. There is a tendency to rush in from work and school, turn on the telly, and crash out. Why not try a new angle? If you have the space, put a comfy chair in the kitchen, so whilst one person is preparing the dinner, another member of the family can sit in and share the events of the day. This stops the whole process being a solitary operation. Just by listening and talking more, it can help you unwind and share the problems of the day.

Try to have a small music system in the kitchen, and look at the preparation process as a way to relax. Let's face it, we have to eat, so why make it hard on yourself? To take things one step at a time we have broken this chapter in a few easy to follow categories.

Equipment

As with any tools that we mention in the book, it is a false economy to always buy the cheapest. Try to buy the best quality you can afford, and you will in return get years of service as long as you look after them. I still have a set of Gustav Lorenze knives that I had way back at college! There are some pieces of equipment that we have found invaluable in our way of life. Rather than go over every item, we have listed them as a tick list and make reference to them elsewhere.

A chest freezer helps to store surpluses and aids buying in bigger quantities.

A large range of pans – the best you can afford. Solid bottomed ones will aid better cooking and result in easier washing up!

A set of kitchen knives containing 2 sizes of chopping knife, a butcher's knife, a carving knife, a small paring knife and a fish filleting knife.

Colour coded chopping boards to help prevent cross contamination and strong flavours being passed from dish to dish.

A food dryer is a great way of storing excess soft fruits and making your own sun-dried tomatoes.

A salad spinner not only improves the taste and texture of your salads, but is a great way to dry blanched vegetables for freezing.

A bread machine – if you're not brave enough to make it the traditional way you can still enjoy the great taste and smell of home-made bread.

A large selection of re-sealable plastic containers to hold a large selection of crops and food to freeze. Cheaper ones will not last long.

A food processor will help with many recipes, especially turning your extra vegetables into great tasting soups.

A microwave, if used correctly, can save time and effort. Don't try to cook every meal in i, but see it as a labour saving device.

A juicer is essential for those tasty and healthy juice drinks (see J for Juicer).

This is not a definitive list, but it will help you get the best from your home grown produce, and will save you money.

MASTERING THE BASICS

We very rarely use recipe books. Don't get us wrong, they have their place for added inspiration for that big dinner party, but only cooking dishes that you find in them can lead to great waste. Currently in this country we throw away 8.3 million tons of food

a year! With a good basic knowledge you can cut down considerably on what you throw away:

- Buy as little pre-prepared food as possible
- Don't be tempted by offers if you won't use them
- Look at what is in your fridge and use up leftovers to create dinner
- Cut down on trips to the supermarket

It is true that the range of food that you can buy from your local supermarket is huge, but we can be easily led into buying products that are sometimes unnecessary. For example, why do they package frozen grated cheese, packet white sauce mix, gravy mix, and pasta sauces when you can make them yourself.

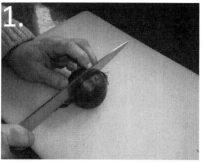
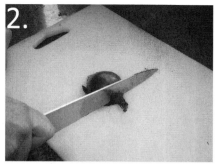
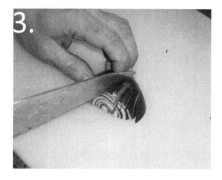

If you can learn a new skill on a regular basis, you will hopefully start to see that cooking is not a chore, and can be very enjoyable as well as therapeutic. Our approach to cooking does not follow a weighed, exact recipe-based approach. As you practice you can build upon our guidelines and set the amounts of individual ingredients to match your own tastes.

MASTERING ONIONS AND GARLIC

Very few savoury dishes are prepared without onions. Unlike other vegetables, onions and garlic have a particular requirement for preparation, so we have included a guide to help you master your knife.

1. Cut the onion in half through the top and the root.

2. Place it on the flat, cut side and trim off the top. Peel off the outer layers of dry skin, exposing the onion beneath.

3. To slice it, hold the onion so that the root end is out to the side, and cut thinly from the top to the root.

4. For chopped onion, place it with the root furthest away from you and slice into the onion up to the root from one side to the other. Then turn the onion so the root is to the side and cut horizontally from bottom to top, finally cutting through, as for slicing.

Garlic is easier, but using fresh is much more flavoursome than preprepared.

Separate the appropriate number of cloves from the garlic. Remove any excess 'papery' skin and place on a board. With the back of a heavy chopping knife, lightly squash the clove. This will enable you to remove all of the skin.

Remove the small root and chop. If you need a paste to cook with, sprinkle some salt onto the chopped garlic and crush it with the back of the knife. You can use a garlic crusher, but we feel these waste too much, and are a fiddle to clean afterwards.

BASIC SAUCES

A basic sauce is the cornerstone to so many different dishes, and once your confidence grows you will become quicker and quicker, and you will develop new ways in which to use sauces in your daily cooking.

WHITE SAUCE

This has so many uses, from lasagne to fish pies, and tasty chicken dishes to jacket potato toppings.

*Equal amounts in weight of
butter and flour (2oz)
1 pint of hot milk
Salt and white pepper*

• Melt the butter in a pan and stir in all the flour using a wooden spoon. If you add a drop of water to the pan this will stop the butter burning before it melts.

• Make sure all the flour is mixed in and keep stirring for a few more minutes to ensure the flour is cooked.

• Add the milk a little at a time and use a whisk to ensure it is incorporated.

- Keep adding the milk till you have the right consistency. It should coat the back of a spoon. Season to taste

- You now have a basic sauce with which to create some additional dishes. For lasagne add some grated cheese. To top jacket potatoes you can add any of your favourite ingredients such as cooked bacon, fried mushrooms, or tuna.

- Or why not add some of your own vegetables finely chopped into the sauce, and simmer for an additional topping.

- You can add leftover chicken to the sauce, ensuring that you heat it thoroughly, and serve it on pilau rice, or with noodles.

TOMATO SAUCE

Next time you are in the supermarket look at the price of stir-in sauces. Like us you may have a surplus of tomatoes, and what better way to use them than to make your own sauces.

This thick, rich sauce can be used to spread on your own pizzas, or mixed with your own favourite pasta to make a tasty and inexpensive dinner.

*Tomatoes (preferably plum,
if you grow them).
Red onions
Garlic
A selection of garden herbs (basil,
oregano, thyme, bay leaves)
Seasoning*

- Pre-heat your oven to gas mark 5. Cut the tomatoes in half and place them in a large, deep baking tray with the roughly chopped onions and whole cloves of garlic. Don't worry about the exact amount of each; the more times you make this sauce you can adjust the proportions to suit your own tastes. Add the roughly chopped herbs and cook until the tomatoes are softened and there is little juice left.

- If there is an excessive amount of water coming from the tomatoes, drain it off into a separate jug.

- Let the mixture cool, then place in your food processor and chopped to a fine paste. You can water it down with any juice taken off during cooking if it is too thick. Put a cupful into individual freezer bags, label, and freeze. The remaining juice can form the base of a soup or a great vegetable stock.

- As well as making the perfect base for your own pizzas it makes a great stir-in sauce for pasta, and can also be served with fillets of white fish or chicken.

- Why not experiment and roast a selection of your favourite vegetables in some olive oil, and add the sauce just as you serve them up.

ROASTING GRAVY

It seems a shame that whilst we spend a lot of time and money on a big roast, many people end up using packet gravy. There really is no need

because we all have the ingredients in our kitchen to make really tasty gravy.

Whatever joint of meat you are roasting, always place it on a bed of vegetables. These should include onions carrots, garlic, celery, and bay leaves.

Don't worry if you haven't got all of them. It's a great opportunity to use whatever you do have. You can replace the onions with leek tops, or use those little onions that are not storing well. Add a drop of water to stop them burning. Fifteen minutes before the meat is fully cooked, pour off the juices and all the vegetable pieces into a saucepan. Skim off any excess fat and bring to a simmer.

You may want to add colour with a little Bovril or Marmite. Simmer for ten minutes and strain into a pan.

Check the seasoning, and you should now have perfect gravy.

The same principal applies to making stews and casseroles.

BASIC STEW

Collect together as many root vegetables as you have and chop them roughly. Flour and season your diced meat. Heat a small quantity of oil in a large saucepan and, when hot, carefully add the meat and stir over a high heat till it has sealed and turned brown. Remove from the pan and add the vegetables. Stir constantly until they start to brown, then return the meat to the pan.

You can add some of our rich tomato sauce that we mentioned earlier, and a pint of stock (see chicken stock in the following category.) Let this simmer on a low heat until the meat is well cooked and tender.

The length of time required will vary depending on the cut, but speak to your local butcher regarding the best cuts he has on offer. He should be more than willing to give you advice on particular different cuts and their cooking times.

Just before serving, season according to taste, and serve with a big chunk of home-made bread.

BASIC STOCK

You may feel that time is too precious to start making your own stock, but it really needn't be a chore. Not only will it save you money but you will be using an additive free tasty ingredient to help flavour up your soups, stews and sauces.

There is no hard and fast set of ingredients, so as with previous recipes, don't feel you have to weigh exact quantities. With time you will experiment and start to use ingredients that you have and like. For this recipe we are making a chicken stock, but it can also be made with beef bones. To achieve a rich colour for beef stock we suggest you roast the bones first. For a fish stock do not simmer for more than 10 minutes.

Bones (as many as you can fit in your biggest pan)
A selection of roughly chopped veg
(can be trimmings) including leeks, carrots, onions, and celery
Bay leaves
Black peppercorns

Add all the ingredients to a large pan and cover with water.

Bring to the boil and simmer for an hour.

Strain and return the liquid to the pan, simmering until the liquid has reduced by half.

Let it cool and then place it in the fridge overnight.

Remove from the fridge and skim of the fat.

You can then freeze it in small containers, labelling and dating them.

BONING A CHICKEN

The difference in price between a whole chicken and one that has been portioned is considerable. Many people feel apprehensive about trying to cut up a whole chicken, but with some guidance and practice it really is quite straight forward.

It is essential that you have a strong, sharp knife, and a suitable chopping board. We recommend that you keep a separate board for all raw meat and fish to reduce the chance of cross contamination.

Firstly, get a plastic tray on which to

71

place your cut up chicken. Then:

1. Lay the chicken on its side and slide the knife under the leg, pulling the leg to the side as you cut.

2. Pull the leg fully over so that you can cut through the joint and remove it. Turn the chicken over and do the same on the other side.

3. Place the chicken with the breast upwards and pull the flesh tight between your fingers. Place the knife to one side of the breast bone and guide it down, as close to the bone as possible.

4. Pull the meat from the bone with one hand till the entire breast is free.

5. Next cut through the wing bone joint.

6. Repeat this with the other side of the chicken.

7. Cut through each leg at the joint to divide the leg and thigh into 2 pieces.

It will certainly take practice, but don't be afraid of having a go. If there is some meat left on the bones don't worry; when you make your stock with them, remove the excess meat from the carcass once fully cooked and use it as another meal.

You can make a stir fry for two with one breast, together with some vegetables and noodles.

Make sure you sanitise all your equipment, work surfaces and especially your hands immediately after you have completed the job!

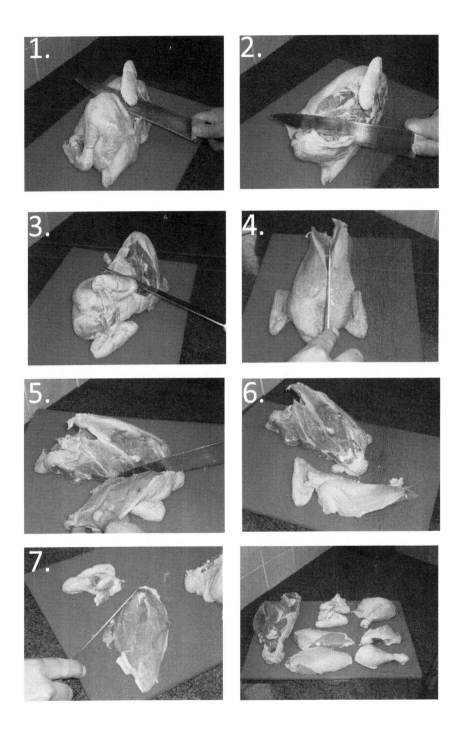

THRIFTY TIPS

Mark your kettle clearly to indicate the amount of water you need to make tea or coffee. This saves on both water and electricity.

Use the oven twice by planning your cooking so that when the oven is on for dinner you also use it to cook something else like bread or a pie.

Double up so that if you are making a lasagne, double the ingredients and make another one for the freezer.

Own brands are usually cheaper. When you shop, try buying these less expensive own brands.

Stale bread should never be binned. Use it to make your own breadcrumbs, or try making a bread and butter pudding.

Use it, don't bin it by keeping a close eye on what's in your fridge, and make sure that you plan dinner around what you have so it is not wasted.

Clear out the freezer every now and again, using up all those meals that you have put in the freezer. It will help you save on buying that week.

Get to know your butcher who will help you with new cuts of meat and ways to cook them to save you money.

Loyalty cards are worthwhile if you use the same supermarket each week. Take advantage of their loyalty card scheme, but be prepared to shop around.

For more help visit **www.lovefoodhatewaste.co.uk** for more advice.

A Well Stocked Larder			
Dried pasta	Rice	Tinned fish	Pulses
Seasonings	Spices	Nuts and seeds	Oils
Start to build up a good stock of these items, and on a week when you need to buy less, why not purchase more items to build a back up for harder times?			

For more help visit **www.lovefoodhatewaste.co.uk**

Livestock

If you ask people what being self-sufficient means, many will answer that it involves keeping an array of animals in their back garden. This perhaps should not be your first step, as keeping livestock comes with a multitude of responsibilities.

However, we are aware that many people are now interested in what keeping animals entails. With this in mind we have included this chapter giving some basic pointers that you may wish to consider before making any purchases. Also, do some additional research through specific books or websites in connection with any particular animals you may be considering.

HENS

The main reason people have for keeping hens is to have their own fresh supply of eggs. Many think they can just keep five or six hens in a hen house and they will be rewarded with a continuous supply of tasty eggs. It's actually never quite that simple, and that goes for all livestock!

Information on the welfare of hens can be found on the Defra website. Make sure you have enough space for them as they should be kept outside with access to a coop or shed, fresh water, and the company of their own kind.

It is advisable, depending on your location, to contact your local Council too to be sure that you are allowed to keep hens on your property. You should also check with your neighbours - just in case.

Consider the type of bird you want to keep. Different breeds will have different characteristics. The best way is to speak to local suppliers and ask their advice, or get onto one or more of the chicken keeper forums and speak directly to others.

You may decide to re-home a few battery hens. From experience this can be very rewarding; they do need a lot of TLC to begin with, but once fit, they are great hens, and you will become very attached to them!

Before you bring any birds home, consider the set up costs before deciding that you will save any money on buying eggs.

That said, keeping chickens is the first step (and often the only step) to keeping livestock, and is certainly growing in popularity.

Your basic requirements will be:

- A hen-house.
- An enclosed run area fenced in with chicken wire.
- Nest boxes to encourage the hens to lay in one area.
- A drinker and a food hopper to dispense feed and water.
- Feed
- A grit container to help with egg production and digestion, unless they are left to free range all day, in which

case they will pick up enough grit naturally.

You will also have to worm our birds regularly, and maintaning a clean coop and surroundings is also a requirement.

If you are considering keeping your hens for meat, the day will eventually arrive when you have to slaughter some birds. The Humane Slaughter Association runs courses on how to kill birds with a minimum of distress, o alternatively, look on the Internet for a list of local abattoirs.

PIGS

Keeping pigs is very different to chickens; mainly you are keeping them solely for meat (although you can keep a pig as a pet). Pigs can be responsible for the spread of foot and

mouth disease and swine flu, so you must contact your local council and Defra before you make your purchase.

Pigs cannot be left to fend for themselves, and require a well balanced diet supplied twice a day. They also need clean fresh water, so make sure you can get water to them for twelve months a year.

They need strong fencing as they love to explore and roam, and should not be kept as solitary animals as they are very sociable.

It would be advisable to take a pig-keeping course which will help you realise if keeping pigs is for you. They will cover many important aspects such as:

• How close is your nearest vet who can help with pigs?
• How will you collect your pigs, and how will you transport them to be slaughtered?
• Do you have enough land and the correct shelter?
• What breed is best for you?
• How will you look after your pigs when you go on holiday?
• How to spot illness.
• What do I feed my pig?
• Where is your nearest abattoir?

Lastly, strongly consider that you may, at slaughter time, have become very attached to your pigs. As you bought your pigs to fatten them up for meat, it usually means that they weren't good enough to breed from. Consider this when purchasing your pigs. Should you become attached, you may need to buy pedigree animals for breeding purposes.

GOATS

Like pigs, goats should not be kept as solitary animals. They also require a good, solid shelter from the elements (goats dislike rain!) and also need a constant supply of clean, fresh water. Goats have been known to die from thirst rather than drinking dirty water.

Consider what you want from your goat, whether it is meat and / or milk. This will help you choose the ideal breed before you buy. Like most livestock, check with your local Council and Defra before buying.

Goats need a good space to roam, and you should be aware that they will browse through hedges and cause havoc in an orchard. With this in mind, make sure you have ample, well fenced pasture.

Check their paddock for poisonous trees and plants too. Any that are poisonous to sheep and horses will also be poisonous to goats. As a rule, evergreen trees are either fairly poisonous or can be fatal. If you keep a small herd they will not need much work, perhaps no more than an hour a day, and will not only supply milk, but also good compost for the garden.

SHEEP

As with other livestock, before you buy your first sheep, ask yourself some questions:

• Do you want to keep them for meat and/or wool?
• Do you have enough land (10 sheep per acre)?
• Which variety should you keep?
• Can you transport them?
• Who could shear the sheep?
• What medical care do they require?

It's a good idea to do some research, and speak to farmers who keep sheep to discus the pros and cons. Offer your time in return for some invaluable working experience. Find out the common ailments they can suffer from, who will help you at lambing, and where the nearest vet is. Again, speak to Defra for some good, sound advice.

BEES

The main reason for keeping bees is pretty obviously honey, but making it profitable is unlikely. As well as giving you a supply of honey (approximately 50lb per colony per year), bees will help pollinate your garden. There has been a steady decline in pollinating insects, so this reason for keeping bees can be very important.

Honey can replace sugar in many recipes, and will be a great bartering tool for other things that you need, but perhaps cannot produce.

Keeping bees means that you will get stung every now and again, so if you or anyone in your family has an allergy to bee stings, it may not be advisable to keep them. Also, depending on the size and location of your garden, think about your neighbours as your colony will certainly not respect any garden fence.

Before you decide to keep bees, speak to your local Beekeeping Association (BKA), and find someone close to you who has a colony and can give you some practical advice.

To start with your hive should only take about an hour per week in summer, and this time will decrease with the onset of winter and experience. Look on the Internet, in books, and magazines to get a feel for the level of knowledge and commitment you will need.

A list of essential equipment includes;

- Protective clothing
- Hive tool
- Smoker
- Hives
- Bees

Keeping animals can be very rewarding, and they can give everyone, especially children, a real connection with nature and where their food originates from, but they do take up a lot of time, and your freedom to go out and about or on holiday will be severely curtailed because your animals will need feeding and locking away every night. If you are seriously considering keeping livestock, it may also be worth locating a good 'animal sitter' to cover you for any emergencies and days away.

MONEY MAKING

If you are actively looking at making a life change and possibly downsizing, now is the time to look at your current financial position (see the budgeting section). Think along the lines of perhaps creating two or more income streams with the thought that if one idea doesn't earn much one month, you will always have something else to fall back on.

Bear in mind too that there are only so many hours in the day, and it can be a fine balance between doing one or two things well, and lots of things much less well!

To begin with it might be an idea for you to list the skills and interests you have, and to look into whether any of these can be turned into money making ideas. For example, you may be good at sewing, so could you offer an alterations service? Are you interested in photography? Making jewellery? Baking? If you like baking or would like to make any food items at home to sell, you will need to speak to your local Environmental Officer.

The list of opportunities is endless. Take each idea in turn and realistically investigate the possibilities.

It's well worth discussing your plans with those around you as they may see possibilities and pitfalls that you can't. In the beginning look at ideas that won't cost much to start up, especially if you haven't been self -employed before (see Occupational Changes, Chapter 15), as it will enable you to 'dip your toe' in the water without spending a lot of money.

You could also look at the possibility of learning or brushing up on a new skill at night school at your local college. As each idea progresses you will need to look at the local competition to see what their Unique Selling Point may be. You will need to create your own USP as a reason why customers might buy or use your own service.

Be careful about just being the 'cheapest' because if you don't do

proper costings of your materials and time, you may be working for nothing. Don't forget that Google offer free websites for small businesses, and advertising in Parish magazines can be a cost effective way of promoting your services. Whatever your ideas, think niche!

When it comes to finding an accountant, choose someone that you can talk to easily, and get at least three quotes so you will have an idea of how much you will have to pay to have your books done. In most cases it's not worth going to a large firm of accountants if your business is either small or a sideline, as they will have to charge more simply because their overheads are bigger than a self-employed accountant. As for tax **www.hmrc.gov.uk** will be a good starting point for advice. and they also do free courses for PAYE etc.

Lastly, the Internet is a vast resource, but be wary of 'working from home' sites. Some of them will be legitimate, but others won't. As a rule of thumb, never pay an 'administration' fee to find work.

If you fancy doing some freelance work then take a look at **www. peopleperhour.com** and **www. freelancealliance.co.uk** – both sites advertise freelance jobs and **www. freelanceuk.com** gives all sorts of advise about how to run a freelance business.

If working for yourself scares you, look at other ways of earning extra money. It could be getting a part time job. What about taking in a lodger? You can earn up to £4250 per year. See **www.direct.gov.uk** for the Rent A Room scheme. You could look into being a host foreign students by

visiting **www.hosts-international. com** and If you would like to rent out parking space, storage space, rooms etc., take a look at **www. spareground.co.uk**.

Don't forget eBay or ebid. You can always raise some extra cash by having a good declutter!

MAKING MONEY FROM YOUR GARDEN

One of the easiest ways to earn some extra pennies from your garden is to sell your produce from your garden gate and use an honesty box. Obviously, the practicality of this idea will depend on the size of your plot and where you live, and also how much passing traffic you have

and if you think it's feasible to have an honesty box or to have buyers knocking on your door. Last year we began to sell small vegetable plants and home grown flowers from a table just outside our gate, and found it to be a great success in as much as it provided us with enough money to buy our seeds, compost etc. for the coming year, making our vegetable growing completely self-sufficient. The margin on plants is healthy too. You pay pennies for seeds, and if you pot up well and attractively you can sell the plants for pounds.

We are lucky because although we live in a rural area, it is on a school run. We were amazed at the age range of those who did buy from us, and it was a lovely way to meet new people! Garden centres often throw away lots

of plastic pots, so you can always see if they'll let you have any for free. We just left a small amount of change in a plastic box and left all our items clearly priced.

With regard to regulations about garden gate selling, we have contacted both Defra and Trading Standards and neither could see a problem with this type of selling. To be on the safe side it may be advisable to speak to your local Council for advice. As regards income tax, you will pay income tax on your sales if you earn over the personal tax allowance. For more information contact the HMRC helpline on 0845 300 0627, or take a look at their website at **www.hmrc. gov.uk** to learn more.

You need to be sensible about how you set out your display. Don't block pavements, have any trip hazards, or put anything in the way of wheelchair use. If you live on a very bad bend then it would be stupid to encourage people to stop there, and you must take great care to ensure no one can hurt themselves when looking or buying from you. Think about how your display would stand up on a windy day, and don't have anything that might be blown over onto the road or path. Don't be put off by this, just be sensible. We've found it a very enjoyable way of earning an extra bit of money!

Ideas that we are planning to try this year include growing vegetables, herb plants, hanging baskets, and home grown flowers. If you don't like the idea of this type of selling, or it's not practical for you, you may want to think about taking a stand at a local farmers' or WI market, or even car boot sales. There may be opportunities to sell to work colleagues or school mums too.

# NATURALLY

The true definition of natural for me is 'existing in or obtained from nature'. However, we have all been drawn to particular products because somewhere on the label we saw the word 'natural'. In our opinion the definition of natural is that the foodstuff has not been tampered with to enhance its taste, appearance, or longevity.

Salt and some fats are totally natural, but we all know that too much of either is not good for you. The whole debate about what is and what isn't natural could fill all the pages in this book, so for a detailed explanation we suggest you go to **www.food.gov.uk** or contact Defra.

To be sure the produce you are buying is natural, steer clear of processed foods. However, there are some processed foods such as pasteurised milk which are technically not 'natural', but clearly won't be harmful. If foods are treated with processes such as concentration and / or pasteurisation, they should not be described as such as 'natural', but

may be described for example as "pasteurised natural orange juice".

Another example of food processing that is not considered unhealthy is the freezing of fresh vegetables. While the best option is to pick them from your garden and use them straight away, freezing vegetables preserves vitamins and minerals, and makes a convenient way to get your 5 a day all year round.

Many processed foods are made using trans fats (edible fats chemically altered to remain solid at room temperature and not existing in nature). They are also known as partially hydrogenated fats. This manufacturing process makes them more stable than natural fats, and better for higher frying temperatures and longer shelf lives. They're found in many processed and commercially baked foods. Saturated fats (the type of fat found mostly in animal products and some plants), cause high LDL cholesterol levels -- and an increased risk of cardiovascular disease. Sources of saturated fat include beef, lamb, pork, lard, butter, cream, whole milk, and high fat cheese. Plant sources include coconut oil, cocoa butter, palm oil, and palm kernel oil. Processed foods are also more likely to contain high levels of salt and sugar.

Processed meat and meat products are some of the worst offenders. They can increase heart problems, colorectal, kidney, and stomach cancers. Though unproven, it seems clear there must be a direct link between the huge increase in fast and convenience foods and the soaring rise in obesity.

The simplest way to avoid any complication could be to look for food that is unprocessed or organic. You may say that this is overpriced and offers very poor value for money when you are doing your fortnightly shop, but we have found otherwise.

If you study the contents of pre-packed food, compared it with unprepared organic and you will be surprised. Not only is organic food not artificially processed, it is produced without the use of pesticides and growth stimulants, and the animals have enjoyed much better welfare.

Many government reports state that they cannot prove that organic is better for you, but one thing is for sure: that eating food full of artificial ingredients certainly can't be.

It is a known fact that fat and sugar are as addictive as heroin; they stimulate the same receptors in the brain that make you feel good, and food manufacturers rely on this to keep you coming back for more.

Don't regard food preparation as a waste of time. You have to give your body a well-balanced diet, so try and enjoy the whole food preparation process. Try to consider the following guidelines when you plan your weekly meals;

- Eat less trans fat, saturated fat, and sugar
- Reduce your intake of salt
- Increase your intake of fresh fruit and vegetables
- Eat more fish, especially oily fish
- Make a third of what you eat starchy food, excluding refined varieties

Living as natural a lifestyle as possible does not just revolve around what we eat, although it may be the most important factor. Take a long, hard look around your house and start to notice those 'unnatural' products that you use, but whose side effects you have never stopped to consider.

Although proof seems slow coming forward, there has been much research linking chemicals in the home to different cancers. The most widely publicised is the link between breast cancer and solid packed air-fresheners. Many polishes and cleaning products are also suspected of causing harm through breathing in vapours (see Cleaning Products).

Some people also make a connection with dropping fertility rates and the way we live our lives today. To conceive both sexes need to be as healthy as possible. Foresight is a charitable organisation which outlines and advises on how to make sure that prior, during and after pregnancy you are all as healthy as can be. Visit **www.foresight-preconception.org. uk** for more information.

We don't want to scaremonger, but it seems we don't know or don't want to know what really goes into the manufacture of products that we are all too keen to put either on or in our bodies. As an example we are taking just one chemical used in many everyday items. Sodium launeth sulphate is generally listed as SLS. This chemical can be found in most shampoos, shower gels, toothpastes, and soaps. Unlike other chemicals it easily passes into the blood stream, even from an application on the skin.

It has then been found to build up in the heart, liver, brain, and lungs, due to the fact that so many products use it. Its primary purpose is to act as a detergent and foaming agent.

To become mild and gentle SLS undergoes a manufacturing process called ethoxylation. This process uses ethylene oxide, a known carcinogen.

It can sometimes seem that we take more care of our cars than our bodies. However, if big companies hide the contents of their products behind big words and e-numbers, we should not just accept that all is well. Whilst we are not saying that there is definitive proof they will harm you, we are saying that not being aware of what we may be doing to our bodies is perhaps a naïve approach to living a full and healthier life.

Try and take that little extra bit of time and effort to check the labels of the products that you bring into your house. You will be surprised how much better it makes you feel.

OCCUPATIONAL CHANGES

As much as we would like to, we can't just throw in the towel at work and start living a self-sufficient lifestyle without some serious thinking. Bills still have to be paid, the house still has to be funded, and mouths have to be fed.

The idea of this chapter is to throw some light onto the choices we do have; choices that were not readily available a few generations ago. So we shall look at two angles of approach that you might consider if you want to feel more in control of your career.

BECOMING SELF-EMPLOYED

A desire to become self-employed suggests that you have a skill or trade that may lend itself to being your own boss. Look closely at others who offer the same services to see how they go about it, and what they charge. Remember, it's no use offering a service which is already over supplied. You have to find a gap in the market by being better, different, or unique.

TRAINING

You may have skills derived from a hobby such as gardening or DIY, but you may need to think about additional training to increase your knowledge. Information about this can be readily found on the Internet or through local colleges for evening or part time courses.

MONEY

Look closely at your outgoings (see Budgeting), and be realistic with any forecasts about what your business might achieve. Not even the best businesses will take off quickly, so cash flow will be crucial in the early days. Many people set up a business using redundancy money, or invest their savings in order to make a dream come true. Make sure that you have enough backing to keep you going through the first year, and be aware of any tools, marketing, stationary, and material costs that you will need to set up.

HOW TO TRADE

You will need to set up your business as one of the following:

Sole trade: basically working on your own

Partnership: as a sole trader, but involving two or more people running the business

Limited Company: this is a more involved legal identity, and is more costly and complicated to set up, but it does keep you completely separate from the business.

If you are not sure, speak to an accountant who will discuss the best option for your particular business. Whichever option you choose you will need to keep accurate financial records. This sounds more daunting than it actually is, and really involves the writing down of purchases and income relating to the business. Again, speak to your accountant and they can draw up a template for you. It's worth getting into the habit of being organised with your books because an accountant will charge you more if they have to spend a long time trying to decipher what you have done!

WHERE TO WORK FROM

There can be a temptation to find premises to work from, but if you can do it, try to work from home. This is not possible in some cases so check with your local Council, mortgage, and insurance company to check you are not breaking any agreements. The advantages are not only financial, but you will save money on rent and rates, and time and money in travelling, and keeping the balance in your new lifestyle may be easier to manage. Although working from home does require self-discipline, and you will need a room where you can shut yourself away from family distractions.

INSURANCE

Check that your current property insurance will cover your new plans. If you are going to use the family car for working you will also need to include it for business use. We also strongly recommend public liability insurance. This will cover you against any claim from a member of the public against damage, or as a result of any work you have carried out.

Above all, be realistic and do not expect to become a millionaire overnight. You won't be able to phone in sick anymore and still get paid, there is no more paid annual holiday, you can't blame your work mates for things not going well, and the office Christmas party can be a very lonely affair! However, the feeling of developing your own business and the satisfaction it brings can be very rewarding.

IS IT TIME FOR A CAREER CHANGE?

You may feel that working for yourself

is not for you, but still want a change in career, so what are your options?

As with becoming self-employed, a career change needs to be well thought out and planned. Ask yourself how satisfied you are with your present career; do you only want to change your current job title, your employer or your complete career?

If it's a lack of motivation you feel then there may be scope to move to a different department or skill sector with the same employer.

You may find that your current employer is open to allowing you (depending on your career) to do some of your work from home. However, the fact that you are reading this book means that you probably want to change the balance between work and home.

To change career completely, think long and hard about the job you want to do. Do you have transferable skills, or will you need to re-train whilst you are in your current job? Be realistic with time scales, and ask those around you who know you best what they think might suit you.

For an unbiased, helpful and professional opinion visit **www. nextstep.direct.gov.uk** (0800 100900). Next step provides information and advice to support adults in making appropriate decisions on a full range of learning and work opportunities. At the time of writing the service was free to all adults in England, and is delivered by qualified careers advisors. We have spoken to them whilst researching this book and the service is very helpful and comprehensive. They arrange a call back consultation, or if you prefer you can book a face to face meeting. This will cover everything, including finding a career that suits your needs, skills, personality and aspirations, as well as putting together your CV and drawing up an action plan.

Be brave and believe in yourself, and that you can take that first big step to balancing the career you need with the way of life you desire.

PRESERVING

In the UK we cannot grow all we need throughout the whole year. So it is important in terms of being self-sufficient, that we look at ways of preserving our crops for use during the winter months when there is little coming from the garden, and also how we can get the most from the food that we do have to buy.

THE FRIDGE

The temperature of your fridge should be kept between zero and 5 degrees Celsius, and always follow the instruction labels.

All meat, poultry and fish should be kept covered, and raw items must be kept in a sealed clean container on the bottom shelf to avoid contaminating cooked meat products.

Leftovers should be cooled then covered, and in the fridge within 1-2 hours. Cooked rice must be eaten within one day, but other food can be eaten within 2 days. Don't reuse tin foil if it has been covering meat, poultry, fish, or rice.

Remove all plastic packaging from fruit and veg, if shop-bought. Carrots, leafy greens, radish, cucumber, corn, beans, and asparagus are best kept in the bottom drawer of your fridge. Broccoli, cauliflower, and celery will keep fresh for longer if you store them in a little water in the fridge.

Berries, grapes, apples, lemons, and limes are all best kept in the bottom drawer of the fridge.

THE FREEZER

Always freeze food by the 'use by date', and use it within one to two days once it has been defrosted. Don't forget to label and date food as you freeze it, especially leftovers so you know what you are defrosting! Cook all food from the freezer until it is piping hot. Meat and poultry can be refrozen once they have been cooked.

www.storingandfreezing.co.uk offers good advice on storing food.

STORING AND FREEZING VEGETABLES

As you gain more experience of growing your own, it will become easier for you to know how much and what varieties of vegetables your family like to eat. The trick is to grow and store enough of your produce to take you through the year.

ROOT VEGETABLES

These can be stored in the ground until you need them, but they will need to be dug up before they get too big and woody. If you look at growing different varieties of a particular vegetable it is possible to sow fewer seeds at one sowing, but to sow at different times of the year. Carrots are a good example of this, and it is possible to be harvesting fresh carrots for most of the year. If you have root crops in the ground in late summer / autumn, cover the soil with about a foot of straw to trap air and to keep the water out.

Apart from parsnips which can withstand frosts, all other root vegetables do need to be dug up before the ground freezes. Neither potatoes nor sweet potatoes can be left in the ground. Once you have dug up your crop, brush off the dirt, but don't wash them. Cut the tops off and remove any that are less than perfect, which can be used straight away rather than being stored.

Take a wooden box and cover the

base with old newspaper, add some moist (but not wet) sand, add the vegetables, and then cover with more sand. Store your box somewhere cool and dry. Don't forget to keep an eye on your vegetable stores and remove any veg that looks less than perfect.

FREEZING VEGETABLES

The best time to pick and freeze your vegetables is whilst they are young and sweet. Only use those that are in tip top condition. All vegetables will need to be blanched before being frozen in order to kill off the enzymes in the vegetables to stop them deteriorating.

To blanch them get a large pot, add some salt to the water, and bring to the boil. Prepare your vegetables by cleaning and cutting them to shape. Add them to the boiling water and boil for the recommended time (see the chart), then plunge them into ice cold water and leave them to cool.

Once cooled, dry them with a clean towel. Freeze vegetables straight away on trays so they do not stick together. Once frozen, place them in freezer bags and get as much air out as you can. Work on the basis of 4oz (100g) per person, per portion, and don't forget to label and date each container.

It is best to blanch and freeze smaller amounts more often, rather than to do large quantities, as you will find it easier to get the vegetables frozen quickly, which will help to keep them in the best condition.

STORING ONIONS AND GARLIC

Make sure that you lift your crop on a warm, dry sunny day, and follow advice on the seed packet. Brush off any excess mud and lay them out to dry completely on wire racks or a patio etc. Make sure that they don't get rained on. It will take a few weeks for them to dry off properly.

If you have any soft onions, or any garlic that has started to sprout, separate these as they won't store well. You can either eat these first or make some caramelised onion chutney. With what's left you can store both onions and garlic in net bags, or you can use old tights. Simply cut the tights into two legs, place the onions / garlic in the foot and knot. Then keep adding and knotting as you go to keep the bulbs separate! The best way to store your 'legs of onions' is by hanging them up in a cool shed. Just cut off an onion as you need it .

BOTTLING

Bottling has been used for many generations to preserve food, but please read the paragraph on botulism before you start. It's not meant to scare you, but you do need to be aware of it.

BOTULISM

Botulism is a very serious, and even

lethal illness, caused by bacteria called clostridium botulinium which can result from eating bottled foods that have not been prepared properly. The problem is that these bacteria can survive in boiling water. They are tasteless, colourless, odourless, and invisible to the naked eye.

The main areas for concern are low acid foods such as vegetables, seafood, meats and sauces.

For this reason we have not covered bottling these items in this book. High acid foods such as fruit, pickles, sauerkraut, jams, jellies, marmalades, and fruit butters will not support the growth of clostridium botulinium, and can be safely bottled at home in boiling water. Tomatoes are a borderline case and need vinegar or lemon juice adding for safer bottling. Never eat bottled food if it has discoloured, gone cloudy, or the lid is loose or comes off easily. If in doubt, throw it out!

STERILISING YOUR BOTTLES

It is important that all your equipment is clean, and you will need to sterilise all your bottles, lids and rings. One way to do this is to get a large pot, fill it with water, and let it boil until you have a good rolling boil. In the meantime, wash your items in hot soapy water and rinse. Once your water is boiling well, place the bottles, lids and rings into the water using tongs, making sure that they are completely submerged for at least 5 minutes. Remove all items and place the jars and lids upside down on paper towelling ready to use. Don't have them standing around for too long before you use them.

Equipment Needed:

A large preserving pan or a galvanised bucket big enough to have a false bottom such as a wire rack, and tall enough so that the bottles are completely covered. The bottles must not touch each other, nor the bottom of the pan, as they will crack.

A thermometer – the best ones are those used for making jam.

A long handled wooden spoon for packing the fruit.

Bottling tongs for picking up the hot jars.

Glass jars either with screw on lids or spring clip tops. The spring clip jars have rubber seals that must only be used once. If you soak these in warm water it will make them more pliable for fitting on the lid. Choose the appropriate sized jar for your needs. Jam jars with twist on tops plus integral gaskets can also be used, and can be useful if you are only bottling small amounts. Don't use any glass that has been chipped. You can reuse glass bottles, but always buy new rubber seals and tops each time you bottle. Wash all the jars thoroughly before using.

A wooden surface on which to place hot bottles.

A large baking tray (if you are using the oven method).

A pressure cooker (if you are using this method).

BOTTLING FRUIT

For bottling, the fruit should be firm and not overripe. Do not use any fruit which has been bruised or damaged. Rinse all fruit in cold water. Small fruits may be left whole while larger fruit can be halved or quartered.

APRICOTS, PEACHES, DAMSONS, AND PLUMS

Remove the stalks. These can be bottled whole or in halves, but you will need to remove the stone. With apricots, if you add some of the kernels it is supposed to bring out the flavour. Remove the skins from peaches and apricots by blanching in boiling water until the skin becomes wrinkly. Peel under cold water. Cut the fruit and quickly bottle it with the cut side down to stop it from discolouring.

SOFT FRUIT

Hull strawberries. Their flavour can be enhanced by soaking overnight in warm bottling syrup. Remove the stalks from currants, cherries etc. Keep an eye out for insects on soft fruit, so pick over them carefully. Cherries are low in acid so you will need to add ¼ teaspoon of citric acid to every pint (600ml) of syrup.

RHUBARB

Remove leaves, and wipe and cut into suitable lengths for the jar. Rhubarb will taste and pack better if soaked overnight in warm syrup.

GOOSEBERRIES

Only use unripe fruit for bottling.

APPLES AND PEARS

These will need peeling and coring. You can cut apples into slices or quarters, but they must be put in slightly salted water to prevent discolouration. Wash before blanching. Blanch apples for two minutes in boiling water before packing. Pears and quinces should be simmered in syrup for a couple of minutes before packing.

FIGS

These can be bottled with or without their skins, but add ¼ teaspoon of citric acid to every pint of syrup, and use equal amounts of syrup to fruit.

TOMATOES

The acidity of tomatoes hovers around 4.6pH, which is borderline for foods which can be safely bottled in boiling water. For every pint (600ml) of tomatoes, add 1 tablespoon of lemon juice or ¼ teaspoon of citric acid. Remove the stems and wash.

Tomatoes can be bottled with or without their skins. To remove the skins simply cut out the top where the stalk is attached, simmer in water until the skins begin to go wrinkly, and place them in cold water and remove the skins.

Tomatoes are bottled in brine, so use ½ oz salt (15g) to every 1¾ pints (1 litre) of cold water. If you want to pack them more solidly, remove the skins, cut in half, and pack in the jar adding 1 teaspoon salt and ½ teaspoon of sugar to every 1lb (450g) of fruit.

HOW TO MAKE FRUIT SYRUP

Use 7-8oz (200-250g) of sugar to every pint (600ml) of water. Simply add half of the water to the sugar and boil for about a minute. Once the sugar has dissolved, add the rest of the water. You can use any type of sugar, or try honey or golden syrup.

PACKING THE FRUIT INTO THE BOTTLES.

Rinse the clean jars in cold water, but don't dry them. Pack the fruit and syrup in layers using a wooden spoon to pack the fruit tightly without damaging it. Get rid of any air bubbles along the way by tapping the jar with the spoon. Make sure that the syrup covers the fruit, but leave an inch clear at the top of the jar.

STERILISING THE FRUIT

You can do this either on the hob or in the oven. Using the hob there are three variations; the slow water bath, the quick water bath, or the pressure cooker. If using the oven you can use the moderate oven wet pack method.

SLOW WATER BATH METHOD

• Fill the bottles with fruit and syrup,

making sure that the fruit is entirely covered. If you are using screw cap jars, loosely screw these on. If you are using spring clips, make sure you are using new rubber seals and close them. Use a wire rack in your bucket or preserving pan, place the bottles on this, and cover completely with cold water. Remember that the bottles must not touch each other or the bottom of the pan. Cover with a lid.

• Bring the temperature slowly up from cold to 55° Celsius (130° F) over an hour, and then follow the guide on page 129.

• When the bottles have been kept at the correct temperature for the exact time, remove them and place on a wooden surface to cool. As the bottles cool, tighten up the screw tops.

QUICK WATER BATH METHOD

• Fill the bottles of fruit with hot syrup at 60ºC (140ºF), put the lids on and put them in your pan or bucket, which should be filled with water at a temperature of 38ºC (100º F), and put the lid on.

• Make sure the bottles are completely covered by the water. Again use a wire rack and don't let the bottles touch. The water should be heated to 88ºC (120ºF) over about twenty five minutes. Simmer for the required time and then remove the bottles. See page 129

PRESSURE COOKER

• As long as your pressure cooker is deep enough to take the bottles sitting on a false bottom, you can bottle fruit this way. The cooker must be able to keep a pressure of 5psi.

• Pack the fruit into warm bottles and cover with boiling syrup. Pour I inch (2.5cm) of boiling water into the cooker. Close the cooker lid and keep the vent open until steam appears, then close the vent and bring the pressure up to 5psi. This should take more than five minutes, but less than ten.

• For soft fruit, apples, rhubarb, plums, damsons and cherries, keep the pressure for 1 minute. For apples that are very closely packed, or for halved apricots and half or whole plums, keep the pressure up for 3 to 4 minutes.

• Figs, pears, and whole tomatoes need 5 minutes, and tightly packed tomatoes need 15 minutes.

• Turn the heat off the pressure cooker and leave for ten minutes, then open the vent. Take the bottles out of the cooker and place on a wooden board.

MODERATE OVEN, WET PACK METHOD

You can bottle all kinds of fruits and closely packed tomatoes using this method.

• Pre heat the oven to 150 degrees Celsius (300 degrees Fahrenheit). Use warm bottles and pack in the fruit, covering it with boiling syrup or brine, and leave 1 inch clear at the top of the bottle.

Place the lids on, but don't secure them. Stand them 2 inches apart on the centre shelf of the oven. After the processing time, remove from the oven, secure the lids, and leave for twenty four hours before checking the seals.

Whichever method you use, let the bottles cool completely. To make sure that the seal has worked, remove the screw caps or clips and lift the jars up by the lids. If the lid remains secure then the seal has worked. If it hasn't worked, don't try to reheat that bottle as it will affect the quality of the fruit you are bottling. Just use the contents up within two days. They should be delicious!

Don't forget to label each of your jars, and store your bottles in a well ventilated place which is dry and dark.

FREEZING FRUIT

As with freezing vegetables, only choose firm, unblemished fruit. Don't use any that are damaged or bruised. A good tip here is to buy the best plastic containers you can afford. Although you will spend more in the short term, the containers will last longer and their lids are more likely to fit properly. Also, buy the correct size for your portions.

Bear in mind that most fruit won't look as good once it has been defrosted, but it will still be fantastic for most puds!

The 4 Ways of Freezing Fruit:

DRY FREEZING

This is sometimes called open freezing, and can only be used for small fruit that does not discolour in air, and can be washed whole without breaking the skins. Soft fruits such as raspberries freeze well, and you can freeze strawberries too, although they will be a bit mushy once they have been defrosted, but you can still use them for pies etc.

• Rinse hard fruits in cold water and dry on paper towels. Don't wash soft fruits. Line a baking tray with greaseproof paper, and line the fruits up so they are not touching. Place in the freezer, and once they have frozen, pack them in bags or containers.

• Try to get out as much air as possible from the bags. You may want to vacuum pack them in portions and then freeze. Don't forget to label with the date of freezing. Use the fruit within eight months.

SUGAR FREEZING

This is a good way of freezing soft fruit that will be used in pies. By mixing the fruit with sugar, it draws out the moisture from the fruit, converting it into syrup which covers and protects the fruit.

• Mix 4oz of caster sugar to every 1lb of fruit. Make sure that the fruit is well covered. Store in rigid containers and freeze. Again you want to get out as much air as possible to prevent freezer burn. This will then keep for nine to twelve months.

FREEZING FRUIT AS A PURÉE

Using this method is great for freezing fruit which is overripe, or perhaps not quite perfect quality. After defrosting the fruit may be used for a mousse, jam, pies, or to go with ice-cream or custard.

• Wash the fruit, peel, remove any pips or stones, and cut up into slices then place in a large pan. Add four teaspoons of water to every one pound of fruit. Heat gently until the fruit is soft, then add 3-4oz (85-115g) of caster sugar. Don't let the fruit boil, but stir until all the sugar has dissolved.

• Once it's cooled slightly, blitz it in a food processor, or pass it through a fine sieve.

• Pack the fruit into portions, either in bags or rigid containers. Fruit frozen this way will last six to eight months.

FREEZING IN SYRUP

Fruits which are good for freezing in syrup are those that are not very juicy, or for those that have been stoned and / or sliced.

• Wash 1lb of fruit in cold water, slice, and dry on paper towels. Remove any sections of the fruit that are bruised.

• Add 8oz (225g) of caster sugar to 1pint (600ml) of water, bring to the boil, and stir until the sugar has dissolved. Add the juice of one lemon.

• Layer the fruit in rigid containers and pour over the syrup. Leave some room at the top of the container for the liquid to expand once it has frozen. Label the container and freeze it. This fruit will last nine to twelve months. You might find it beneficial to freeze in portion sizes.

FREEZING CHERRIES

However you decide to freeze cherries, they must always have their stones removed as they become bitter if the stone is left in. Remember to wear an apron as the juice will stain! If you toss cherries in lemon juice before freezing, this will help them keep their colour.

DRYING FRUIT

This is a great way of using up gluts in your crops, and dried fruits make great snacks. There are two basic methods; one uses your oven, and the other uses a food dehydrator. It just depends on how much drying you think you might do.

• To get the best results, choose fruit which is in tip top condition. To stop apples from browning, slice straight into a bowl of water with lemon juice and leave for five minutes. Rinse before you lay the slices out.

• Wash the fruit and slice, making sure that your slices are the same size – ¼ inch thick is ideal, as this will help the fruit to dry evenly. You don't need to peel apples, pears, citrus fruit, or fruit with stones if you don't want to, but you will need to remove the stones and core the apples.

• If you are intending to dry a lot of apples, you may want to consider buying an apple corer as this will save you a lot of time, and you will be able to slice the apples into rings.

• Lay the fruit in a single layer on a baking or wire tray. If you are using the oven, turn the temperature to 130 degrees Celsius (250 degrees Fahrenheit), and leave for a few hours until all the moisture has gone from the fruit. You may want to leave the oven door ajar to help the air flow. The drying process will take anywhere between four and twelve hours. Check the fruit occasionally and turn it over. If you are using a dehydrator, follow the manufacturer's instructions.

• To help keep the fruits' colour you can pre-treat before you dry. Experiment and see which method you prefer.

ASCORBIC ACID

Use five tablespoons of ascorbic acid for every pint of water. This dip is suitable for all types of fruit.

HONEY DIP

Stoned fruits such as plums, apricots, nectarines, and damsons, as well as bananas, can be glazed with a mixture of one part honey to two parts water. Heat the water and let the honey dissolve. Once this has cooled, coat the fruit and leave overnight before starting the drying process. This will help the fruit keep its colour and add a slight glaze.

PECTIN DIP

Add one box of powdered pectin to one cup of water, and bring to the boil. Once the pectin has dissolved, add ½ cup of sugar and stir until this has dissolved. Remove from the heat and add 1 cup of cold water. Dip the fruit straight in as you slice, then lay out on trays to dry. This method is suitable for berries, cherries, and peaches etc.

TIPS FOR BETTER DRYING

• Remove the stone, then turn the fruit inside out. This shortens the drying time.

• Blanche grapes and blueberries in boiling water for 2 minutes. This makes the skins more porous.

• Steam slices of apple, pear and apricot for 5 minutes before plunging them in ice cold water. Leave to dry on kitchen roll.

• Properly dried fruit feels crisp and slightly leathery, and should bend slightly. If there are damp spots it needs more drying.

• Once it is ready, leave the fruit to cool for twelve hours.

STORING DRIED FRUIT

• Place the fruit in air tight containers such as glass jars, plastic zip lock bags, or any other plastic container with a tight fitting lid. You can also pack it layered on greaseproof paper in larger containers.

• Room temperature is best for storing dried fruit, but not in direct sunlight or near a heat source. A cool, dark cupboard is ideal. Given the right conditions your dried fruit will keep for twelve months.

• You can also freeze dried fruit and again it will last twelve months.

COOKING WITH DRIED FRUIT

• Before cooking, soak your dried fruit in cold water. Stone fruits will need at least twenty four hours, and apples and pears twelve hours. Just use enough water to cover the fruit. You can then use the water to cook with. Bring to the boil very slowly and simmer gently until tender.

• Don't add sugar until the fruit is almost cooked, then sweeten to taste.

• This fruit can be used for pies and puddings.

• If you want to rehydrate the fruit before eating, just place it in some water for thirty minutes before using.

QUALITY OF LIFE

Planning to change the way you live will be both exciting and challenging, and you may need to spend some time just thinking and planning before you jump in. If you're single then you only have your own needs and welfare to think about, but if you have a family you will also need to consider their feelings and aspirations as well as your own.

Sometimes making profound changes to your life can come about because you have faced a life changing event, or it could be that you just feel life is not running as you would like it to.

From a personal point of view many years ago, after a turbulent series of events, and having become quite depressed, I found it very helpful to plan out what kind of life I would like to lead – one that would be both achievable and satisfying financially and emotionally. I got a pile of A4 sheets and a pen and sat over a few nights, just planning.

One sheet I called my day dream sheet, on which I wrote down all the things I would like to do regardless of my then current situation, money, qualifications etc. The next sheet, I called my sweet dream sheet, and here I took my original day dreams and tried to repackage them in a more manageable way.

The last sheet was my sunshine sheet on which I listed how I could make my goals practical and achievable within one year, given the situation I was in at the time. I think it is important to have goals, however simple, that you can achieve within a one year period. I then put my sheets of paper away and set to work changing my life. After a year I did look at my sunshine sheet again, and I had achieved the goals that I had set myself, and this gave me a tremendous sense of achievement. You can also refer to your sheets along the way to help motivate you.

No life change is ever easy, but if you break down the changes you want to make into bite sized chunks and list them, you will find that it helps you and your family to stay committed and motivated, because you will be able to tick the things you have attained. Ideally you want to aim to have something to achieve on a month-by-month basis. It doesn't matter how small those changes are. You could also try doing something like this;

The plus side	How it may affect you
Change of job	Possibly less money
Less stress	Feeling more energised
Smaller social circle	Making new friends
Feeling more in control of your life	Need to be more self-disciplined
Less commuting	Feeling healthier

As you can see, the list will go on and will be personal to you and your circumstances, but this just gives you some ideas to start with.

However you want to live your life, feeling that you have some degree of control over it is very liberating, and for us, having a more self-sufficient lifestyle is far more rewarding. You make your own choices and see the direct rewards of your hard work, and save money in the process.

Sure, there are some initial things you may miss, but to be able to decide on a sunny day that work can wait and that you are going to spend a day in the garden is a freedom that we really appreciate.

You will also become less materialistic and enjoy sharing the harvest from your hard work with your new found friends, so try to see that happiness doesn't necessarily come from owning more designer stuff, but rather from a real desire to take control and shape your own life and future.

ROTATION OF CROPS

The basic idea behind crop rotation is to prevent the build up of pests and diseases in your soil. In addition, if you keep growing the same crop on the same patch, it will deplete the soil of nutrients. As already noted, it's worthwhile testing your soil for its pH value.

If you have a larger plot then it's worth doing a few tests in different sections, as you may get different results. Whatever your soil, you will need to add compost and manure to it at least once a year as doing this will help to replenish your soil's nutrients and improve drainage.

If you can, divide up your plot so that you won't be growing the same crop on the same ground for four years. This is because it can take up to four years for soil borne diseases and pests to fall to a level where they become harmless. Ideally you don't want to grow crops on the same patch for more than one season. This is especially important with brassicas (cabbages, broccoli, cauliflower etc.) because if you don't rotate them, they will soon suffer from a disease called 'club root' which deforms the roots of brassicas, and once you get this disease in your soil, you won't be able to grow brassicas again for eight years.

Decide which crops you're going to grow, and draw a sketch of your growing area. We have a rabbit-proofed area that we grow most of our vegetables in, and many years ago we sketched out a 'master' plan which is now photocopied every year and updated.

All the old copies get put into a folder, and this way we can easily see where and when vegetables have been planted. On your plan you could also incorporate two extra sections – one for notes so that you can jot down any ideas that have worked particularly well that season, and also a brief note about how the weather has been.

All this will help you to build up a picture of what works best in your plot as the years go by.

Once you know what you are growing for the season, list them together in their family groups. Planting crops in family groups will make it easier for you to plan your rotation, and you will know what each group requires in terms of nutrients in order to achieve healthy growth.

THE EIGHT VEGETABLE GROUPS

Cabbage family brassicas	*Cauliflower, kale, cabbage, calabrese and broccoli, swede, turnip, radish, land cress, mustard, sprouts, and kohlrabi*	These crops are long growing and thrive best in soil that is rich in organic matter. They also need the soil to have a pH level of 6.5 to 7.0. They should be at the start or at the end of your rotation cycle. They are best planted in the same place as the pea family the previous season.
Potato family solanaceae	*Potatoes, tomatoes, peppers, and aubergines*	Manure should be added to the patch where you are planning to plant potatoes, as they like the soil to be fairly high in nitrogen, and be slightly acidic with a pH of around 5.5. Both potatoes and tomatoes are hungry feeders.
Pea family	*Peas, runner, broad and French beans, fenugreek, clover, and alfalfa.*	These are all light feeders which put nitrogen back into the soil.
Onion family	*All the onion family, plus garlic and leeks*	These are light feeders and should be planted in ground which has previously grown heavy feeders such as the potato family.
Marrow family	*Marrow, pumpkin, courgettes, melon, squash, and cucumber*	These require a lot of room and need well manured soil. Make sure that the manure is at least a year old, otherwise it will burn the plants.
Carrot family	*Celeriac, carrots, parsley, celery, parsnips, and fennel*	Carrots need light, sandy soil with an ideal pH value of 6.5 to 6.8. Having said that, we have found that growing them in large pots with multi-purpose compost gives us the most consistent results.
Daisy family	*Jeruselem artichoke, lettuce, endive, salsify, chicory, and scorzonea*	
Beetroot family	*Beetroot, spinach and spinach beet, Swiss chard, Good King Henry*	Sweetcorn is not part of any family group and can be planted within other crops.

ORGANISING YOUR ROTATION

BASIC CROP ROTATION	
Potato family	Daisy family
Onion family	Marrow family
Pea, bean family	Carrot family
Cabbage family	Beetroot family

Brassicas should be planted in soil that has been previously used for beans and peas. This is because beans and peas put nitrogen back into the soil, which is what brassicas need.

Potatoes need nitrogen, but don't plant them next to brassicas as they need different soil pH values.

Don't plant root vegetables in soil that has had manure in it the previous season because they will grow better foliage than vegetables, and also the vegetables can split if the soil is too rich.

Peas and beans like lime, so add some to the soil before planting.

Nothing about crop rotation is set in stone; if it's impossible to incorporate all of the above tips on your plot, don't worry. The main thing is just to move your crops around. Also, you will find that companion planting will interfere with traditional crop rotation, but you may find the results are worth it. For example, growing carrots and onions together in rows will confuse the carrot fly because of the onion scent.

We also find that growing flowers such as marigolds and herbs etc. within our vegetable plot not only makes it look more natural and colourful, but having a wide variety of plants together attracts beneficial insects, which in turn feed off the not so good insects.

SKILL SHARING

Having made the decision to be more self-sufficient, you will probably need to learn new skills. This process can be both exciting and daunting, so once you have decided exactly what it is about your life that you wish to change, you can then go on to look at the skills that you already have and those that you would like or need to learn. By doing this, you can create your very own step-by-step skill guide.

These days there are plenty of resources at your fingertips to help with your research and learning. The Internet and libraries make good starting points. If you find a really useful book in the library, you may wish to buy your own copy to keep.

If you're interested in finding courses, look in the back of associated magazines such as Home Farmer, Country Smallholding, Permaculture, or search the Internet.

One website that you might want to look at is **www.wwoof.co.uk** which stands for World Wide Opportunities on Organic Farms. This is a charity which teaches people about Organic farming through hands on experience. They have a list of organic farms, smallholdings and gardens which offer food and accommodation in return for some practical help on their land. You are not expected to be knowledgeable about farming, but must be willing to learn and fit in within the host's way of life.

www.justfortheloveofit.org is a site that also may be of interest. Its aim is to bring people together in their local communities by sharing either tools or skills. It's free to join, and no money changes hands between members.

LETS, or Local Exchange Trading System, is a UK and worldwide system where people exchange goods and services with each other without handing over money. To find your local LETS group, go to **www. letslinkuk.net**

Bartering is an old method of exchanging products without cash, and can be used just as effectively with skills as your currency. You may desperately need someone to build

a fence or a wall that you would find hard to do. If you have a neighbour who has these skills, but is in need of someone with your skill set, then do a deal. This also gives you the benefit of watching and learning as the work is being done.

Just remember, you are never too old to learn, and the more practical everyday skills you acquire mean that you will depend less on having to buy in skills, taking you one more step closer to self-sufficiency.

TOOLS FOR THE GARDEN

As with all purchases you should try to buy the best quality you can. This may mean upgrading your current selection of garden tools with better quality ones when money allows you to do so.

If you take a trip to your local garden centre you will find a huge array of gadgets, from leaf blowers to extendable grabbing tools. It all depends on your bank balance, the size of your garden, what you are growing, and how fit and able you are.

Once you have decided on the type of tools you need, speak to friends who may be able to recommend a particular brand. Look at gardening sites on the Internet, and get some feedback from forums. Also go to your local supplier to get their opinion, and try out several before you buy.

Maintaining your collection of garden tools is very important. The better you look after them, the more years of usage you will get. Always try to clean them before you put them away,

as it is disheartening when you come to use them next and they are covered in baked on soil. With cutting equipment, make sure that you regularly sharpen them on a sharpening stone, and keep all moving parts well greased.

Organise your tool shed so you can easily get at them, and keep anything dangerous well out of the reach of children. Make sure that your shed is secure to safeguard against theft too. We have installed a battery operated motion sensor alarm in ours, along with tamper proof locks and large padlocks. You can mark your bigger pieces of garden equipment with one of many invisible markers available and register them online. A deterrent is always the best form of defence, so try to install motion activated lighting outside your shed, but try to set it high enough so that every cat in the area doesn't keep setting it off.

'Must Have' Labour-Saving Gardening Tools

A garden fork for digging and turning soil will have square prongs (tines), whereas a fork for scooping and carrying plant material around the garden will have round prongs.

Spades come in various sizes and weights, but try to buy one with a stainless steel blade. This will prolong its life and make digging easier. The top of the blade where you push it into the soil is better flattened to save on your feet, and although bigger blades will mean less bending, they also increase the weight per dig, so try one for size.

Hand forks and trowels should be robust. Once bent they will not last long. Do not be tempted by very cheap ones.

Hoes should be the right height for you to avoid unnecessary strain on your back. There are two varieties, a push hoe which, as the name suggests, pushes the soil, and the draw hoe which pulls soil towards you.

Rakes come in all shapes and sizes, and cover an assortment of uses, including tidying up autumn leaves, clearing the lawn, levelling soil, or removing stones. Think what you want it to do before you buy. We use two styles; a fine wire rake for collecting leaves, and a shorter, more robust one, for removing stones.

Secateurs vary in quality and price. Get advice from your local garden shop.

Shears are primarily used for trimming hedges and cutting back perennials. Extendable handles are useful.

Bulb planters will dig out suitable sized holes, allowing you to plant bulbs at the correct depth, and with a squeeze of the handle will return the soil, covering the bulb. Essential if you will be doing lots of planting.

Watering cans can be heavy. Try out some different styles.

Gloves, especially well fitting ones, are essential. Choose a pair that will suit your workload.

Wheelbarrows come in mant styles. If you have lots of hawthorn choose a type with a tubeless tyre. Also, make sure it will fit through your gates!

'Must have' labour-saving gardening equipment:

Lawnmowers: there is more choice if you opt for a petrol mower. Seek advice if unsure.

Strimmers: I prefer petrol and plastic blades rather than line, which is bprone to breakage. Follow the manufacturer's safety recommendations, including wearing goggles.

Chainsaw: these require extreme caution and a course to be safe. They are mainly used for cutting down trees and cutting logs to size.

Rotavators: These are motorised diggers, and essential if you have a large plot to prepare, or are starting on a new patch. A rotavator will save many hours and backache and will help turn in manure and aerate the soil. If you don't buy one, consider hiring one.

UNDER PLASTIC

The idea of growing under plastic can stir up mixed emotions with people. The polytunnel has had some bad press due to the acres and acres of some counties now under plastic with commercial growers.

However, 'under plastic' doesn't have to be a polytunnel. We are fortunate and have an eighteen foot long tunnel which it would be hard to live without, but if you have a small patch there are many other ways you can enjoy the benefits of growing under cover. We shall look at alternatives to a tunnel later, but let's look at the benefits and possible problems of polytunnels.

BENEFITS

As opposed to greenhouses, tunnels are far more affordable, especially if you are planning something bigger than eight foot square. A tunnel can cover four times the space of a greenhouse for just a quarter of the price. Also, if you have children there is no possibility of broken glass from a stray football.

In most of the UK we only have a six month window in which to grow our crops. A polytunnel can start spring six weeks early, and delay winter by an additional 4 weeks. This can help with some crops by enabling a second sowing, and with others gives a longer fruiting period.

At the time of writing this you do not require planning permission for a domestic tunnel. If, however, you are in a conservation area you may wish to seek advice from your local planning office. If you are considering a large tunnel over twenty feet, you may, for peace of mind, want to contact them. They are not viewed as permanent structures, but ours has now been up for over ten years.

Using courgettes as an example, we sow two early in late February in heated propagators, and plant them into the soil in the tunnel, a second sowing for outdoors in April to plant out after the frosts, and a third in June for growing in the tunnel again for cropping well beyond the outdoor ones. This works particularly well with courgettes as they do not keep by any

method, and the tunnel gives us an extended harvest.

If you grow hanging baskets, whether flowers or fruit, you can plant them up a lot earlier, and they will be coming towards blooming when the time comes to put them out.

Growing under plastic can also protect your crops from pests such as birds, rabbits, and airborne ones such as carrot fly.

As with a greenhouse, it gives you the possibility of growing tender, sun-loving crops such as melons, cucumbers, peppers and chillies.

If, like us, you want to make some cash from your garden, you can think about growing 'cut flowers' such as chrysanthemums in the spring to sell

at the beginning of winter .

Your plants, and you too, will appreciate the benefits of protection from the wind. The first chance in early February to get out into the polytunnel protected from the elements is a great realisation that the growing season is about to start.

POSSIBLE PROBLEMS

Growing under plastic may protect your crops from some pests, but others such as white fly and red spider mite can cause problems.

You may fall into the trap of growing tomatoes every year in your tunnel, but beware as blight will take a hold and could lower yields. Always have good ventilation throughout the

summer to try to reduce diseases.

Daily watering is also essential as your plants are sheltered from the rain. This can be a nuisance, especially at holiday time, so try to ask a friend or neighbour to look in if you are away.

As mentioned earlier, tunnels can be considered an eyesore, and you may risk upsetting neighbours.

Depending on the quality of the covering that you buy, you will eventually need to replace it when repairs are no longer enough. This can range from once every three years to five or maybe six, but try to buy the best you can.

They can take up a fair amount of space, and care needs be taken when you are considering a site for it.

WHAT DO I BUY?

There are a multitude of different varieties of tunnels that you can buy, but follow these suggestions before you spend your money.

- A wider, shorter tunnel is better than a longer, narrow one
- Make sure the hoops are straight sided for the first 3-4 feet to maximise growing space up to the sides
- Aim for strong galvanised steel hoops that are only 6-8 feet apart
- Buy the best cover you can afford, preferably with anti-fogging covering to stop internal dripping.
- Search the web for assistance. There are many good companies selling polytunnels.

ALTERNATIVES

If you are starting out on your journey of self-sufficiency and don't want to commit to a tunnel yet, there are other ways in which you can grow under plastic. You will still enjoy the benefits of extending the growing season, and have additional crops in the colder months at the end of the year, but you will use less space.

Cloches come in all shapes and sizes, and will protect your plants from early frost. You can place them over the soil prior to planting to warm the soil, enabling you to plant out earlier. They will also protect crops from birds and other pests. However, you will need to gradually acclimatise the plants by removing the cloche on warmer days to avoid them collapsing and dying.

Mini greenhouse cloches cover larger areas than traditional rigid cloches, and are made from sheets of polythene and small hoops. They vary in size to meet specific requirements.

Super cloches are similar to greenhouse cloches, but are generally made from rigid sheets of PVC and have metal clips to ensure extra strength.

Mini garden greenhouses are free standing shelving covered with a plastic over-jacket. We find these invaluable when moving seedlings out of the heated propagators. They first go into the mini greenhouses inside the polytunnel as an additional acclimatisation stage before going into the tunnel, and then hardening off outside.

Bell Cloches are pre-formed plastic bells that can go over individual plants such as courgettes to give them a head start in acclimatising to being planted outside. Make sure that they are tilted to add ventilation, and beware of strong winds (although they can be fixed down with tent pegs).

VERMIN CONTROL

The true definition of vermin is various destructive small animals and insects which are either annoying and / or injurious to health. This can cover a vast selection of flying and creeping insects. In this chapter we will concentrate on those creatures that cause us the most disruption and nuisance.

MICE AND RATS

Mice in the garden are a pain as they love to eat new fresh shoots on emerging vegetable crops. With this in mind we grow our beans and peas in pots, and plant out only when they are at least three inches tall. You can't stop them getting into your vegetable patch, but if you have a holly bush, place a spread of leaves around the base of vulnerable crops to give them a prickly shock.

You may see evidence of mice rather than actual mice in the house. This includes small, dark droppings, chewed boxes, woodwork and cables, a strong, urine-like smell, holes in walls and skirting, and grease marks around cracks and doorways. Mice and rats have to chew as their teeth are constantly growing, and they have to wear them down to avoid starving to death.

Prevention in the house is always better than cure. Walk around the outside of your property and look for any holes, and fill them. A mouse can get through a hole the size of a pencil, so be thorough. Cover air bricks with a fine wire mesh, and check in barns and sheds if they are built up against the house.

Good housekeeping can stop mice having a banquet in your home. Make sure all food is stored in your pantry in sealed containers, and all areas and floors are kept free from spillages and rubbish.

If you have a problem inside your house there are many companies who will lay bait boxes around selected locations. They can also visit your house on a monthly basis to check for any additional evidence, and deal with it accordingly.

Outside you can set bait boxes for both rats and mice. Always follow the instructions before using any poisons in your garden though, and do take into consideration wildlife, pets, and especially curious children.

Rats will generally stay clear of your house, but they will nest around a good source of food. Compost bins can be a favourite, and we have even found them inside the bins, which can be a shock when you lift the lid. Most compost bins stand straight onto the ground, making access to your food scraps all too easy for a persistent rat. To overcome this we place 2 sheets of chicken wire on the ground, place the compost bin on top, and fold the wire over the base. This is then fixed with fence wire twisted tight to keep it in place. This ensures the worms get in, and keeps the rats out!

If you have concerns over rats you can use a professional pest control company. Be aware that as winter draws in, so the mice will consider your house a nice, warm place, so extra care is needed. Regularly baiting poison boxes will control the spread, but remember that mice breed at an incredible rate, so perseverance is essential.

WASPS

Wasps are more a nuisance to us than our homes or gardens. In fact, in the early part of summer they are responsible for eating other destructive insects.

Their real annoyance factor kicks in with the onset of late summer when tree fruits are ripening. They are attracted to the sweetness, so try to pick the fruit as soon as it is ripe.

Hang homemade traps in the garden, but try to keep them away from flowering plants as you may trap bees as well. Tie a bottle or a large jar to a tree half-filled with water and a good helping of jam. Secure a foil cover over the top and make a small opening for the wasps to get in. The smell of the jam will draw them in, but they will be unable to escape.

Wasps like to nest in cool, dark and undisturbed areas like barns, roof timbers, and wood stores. If you find a nest, use professional pest controllers to destroy it. There are nest sprays that you can buy from your local garden store, but be aware that there may be many hundreds of wasps inside.

SLUGS

Slugs are the curse of every vegetable gardener. They are a silent, invisible menace that can butcher your brassicas and level your lettuces.

There are as many potential ways of controlling slugs as there are varieties, and we list some below. As we maintain a healthy organic approach to our garden, we have not included any contradictory ways to see them off.

The most popular trap is the 'slug pub'. This involves a half-filled plastic container with beer buried in the ground next to your vulnerable crops. Attracted by the yeast, the slugs then drown themselves in the beer.

You can prevent slugs from getting to your crops. We cut the tops and bottoms of large plastic milk containers and grow our crops inside them. Slugs do not like the smooth plastic or the jagged edge, and will not climb over.

Other barriers you could try are salt, wood ash, sawdust, or crushed eggshells. There are some pesticide -free ways of creating a barrier, and the most effective is by using copper rings. These carry a positive charge which the slugs hate, but they are expensive and the cost soon adds up if you are growing a lot of brassicas.

Make sure you encourage nature's own attack team, especially birds who love to eat slugs. Beetles will also help to bring the slugs under control as well as parasitic nematodes. These can be bought from garden shops. You simply follow the instructions to eradicate the slugs in their hiding places. And if all else fails you can sit out at dusk and collect them by hand, but we feel life is a little too short for this!

MOLES

Moles do no real damage for the vegetable gardener, but if you are proud of the condition of a beautifully kept lawn, then they can be a real pest. Saying that, they can disturb the root systems of your crops, and they

FOXES

There are strong and opposing opinions on foxes. They are no longer the sole concern of country dwellers, and there are occasions when they enter city homes, and on one occasion caused horrific injuries.

The fox is an opportunist and city living offers the perfect foraging environment. Discarded waste and rubbish bins are an easy target for a hungry fox, and offer far richer pickings than the countryside.

If you keep hens you will be aware of the need to 'fox proof', and the necessity to keep them in at night. They have also been known to take pet rabbits from gardens.

If you don't keep hens the presence of foxes needn't bother you, except for the occasional smell of the males' urine. You may want to get your own back and use male human urine as a deterrent around the areas that you think the fox is coming into your garden. Their presence may deter mice and rats from nesting in your garden.

As with nearly all unwanted visitors to your property, keeping things clean will deter foxes. Keep rubbish sacks in bins, otherwise foxes will rip them open. You can purchase fox repellent from garden shops, but many people enjoy the presence of foxes in their garden and spend hours observing them.

have a huge appetite for worms.

There is no humane, effective way to get rid of them. Unless you gas them, trap them, or shoot them you will find all other methods just deter them for a short period.

If they do not bother you, leave them be as they eat many insects and pests. If you want them gone then your only real way is to use a professional mole catcher who will discuss the most effective way to rid you of your moles.

WATER MANAGEMENT

Water is one of nature's most valuable commodities. Since the privatisation of water, the cost has escalated, and therefore so has the need to be more conscientious in making your consumption as frugal as possible.

In other chapters we have spoken about making the most of your utilities in the house, so in this chapter we are going to concentrate on outdoor usage.

We are one of just a few European countries that has only one quality of water entering our houses. Hence we find ourselves watering lawns, filling ponds, and watering our crops with chlorinated and heavily filtered water. This equates to pouring a very expensive commodity over your garden.

COLLECTION

The average rainfall in the UK is approximately 920mm per year. If your roof is 300 square metres, allowing for a percentage of waste you could collect over 200,000 litres of water every year. That is 200 cubic metres of water, and at the time of writing the unit cost was £1.24 per cubic metre. We are therefore pouring away the equivalent of £248 worth of water down the drain!

To put that into context, we use on average 140 cubic metres of water a year, or significantly less than our roof could supply. Obviously the water from the roof is not fit for consumption, but it is much more suitable for watering our crops and filling our pond. There are many companies who can supply under- or overground storage tanks. If this is something you are seriously considering then it is possible to use this water for flushing toilets and in washing machines, subject to minor plumbing alterations.

If this sounds too big a step, you could simply collect rainwater in water butts from your drain pipes. If you connect 2 or 3 butts together on different levels, water can pour from one to another when full. Make sure you get the biggest you can afford, and that will sensibly sit securely next to your down pipe.

DISTRIBUTION

We are fortunate enough to have a well in our garden that is some 8 metres deep. To harvest this free supply we have submerged a sump pump into the well, securely restrained by stainless steel cable. It is a false economy to buy a cheap sump pump as it will not be able to lift the water to any great height and deliver it around your garden.

We have sunk distribution pipes underground which connect to three different isolating taps around the garden and polytunnel.

Via a series of taps we can fill water butts in different areas without having to make countless trips with a watering can. We scoured the Internet and purchased cheap old drinks storage drums. Once they are fully washed out they make great water storage butts. Because we have a very powerful pump we can connect a hosepipe to the end and water freely with the pressure it delivers.

Not everybody will have a well, but you can purchase smaller water butt pumps and lay underground pipes to achieve the same effect. There is now even a solar-powered one.

In the polytunnel it is worth considering a drip feed system connected to a slightly elevated water storage butt. Nearly all crops grown under cover require 'little and often' watering, and this can save hours of time and the possibility of losing crops. These are stocked in most garden centres and can be cut to fit your own needs. Try not to keep the water butt in the polytunnel as sitting water in the heat of the tunnel will cause rapid bacteria growth and affect your crops. It is worth treating your water butts with a natural cleaner, also widely available from garden centres.

GREY WATER

Grey water is the waste water that comes from sinks, showers, washing machines, and baths. There are mixed feelings about using grey water to water your crops, and our opinion is to avoid it if you can.

It is important that if you are going to use grey water then you should not store it for more than a couple of days as it will start to smell and go rancid. Also, you will have to use only biodegradable cleaning products to avoid contaminating your land.

You will also need to know what is going down your sink. If you do a lot of frying, then you will have high levels of fat and consequently detergent in with your grey water, and this will not be beneficial to your crops.

With all this in mind and the need to reroute waste pipes, it may be better to spend your time and money collecting clean rainwater.

HELPFUL HINTS

If you ask 5 different gardeners when to water your plants, you will

122

probably get 5 different answers. As a guideline, try to water first thing in the morning and late in the afternoon. This will save losing a lot of water to evaporation.

Try to make sure that you mulch your plants. This can be done with leaves, bark, or straw. Not only does it retain water in the soil, it also helps reduce the growth of weeds.

You can also use large plastic drinks bottles filled with water and stuck into the soil upside down next to your plants to ensure a steady watering.

Try to avoid sprinklers. They are a time-saver, but they can waste a lot of water by spraying it into the air rather than on the soil.

Try looking on the Internet for large containers to use as water butts. Some drinks manufacturers sell large containers that can be drilled and fitted with a tap.

Be aware that different vegetables and fruits have different watering requirements, so make sure that each plant gets the right amount.

XPERIMENT

OK! We admit it's a little tenuous, but finding a self-sufficient word beginning with X was always going to prove difficult!

As we have said from the very beginning, becoming totally self-sufficient is virtually impossible, but any degree of success you have will be based on your ability to experiment and improvise. So take on the challenge, combining experimentation with a hint of realism.

We try to do as much as is physically possible. By growing, cooking, making, fixing, recycling, selling our produce, foraging, bartering, and watching what we buy, we are getting as close as we can without it taking over our lives.

With all our recipes, methods, plans, and way of living, you can experiment for yourselves to find the level of self-sufficiency that best suits you.

Don't be afraid to have a go either. As with all wisdom, knowledge, and experience, you can only achieve better and better results by trying and seeing what works in practice, and what doesn't.

Try to experiment with the following:

• With what you eat – it will improve your health and should be fun too.

• With what you buy, and save a small fortune on those things you don't really need.

• With what you grow, and taste food the way nature intended.

• With your essential purchases by looking at alternative suppliers, and more cost effective products.

Above all, have fun along the way, and don't be scared of making mistakes.

YEAR PLANNING

Most of us are creatures of habit, and breaking with a well established routine can be difficult. We tend to do things at the last minute, and this can mean that you pay more for your purchases, or even find that things are no longer available when you actually want them.

What we are covering in this chapter is the planning of all those jobs and purchases you need to do, so you get the best product for the best price. As you will see, it can save you hundreds of pounds a year.

When things are at their highest demand, they are usually also at their highest price. The classic example of this is holidays when schools have broken up for the summer. Some things will be difficult to avoid, but with a little planning, a considerable sum of money can be saved.

If like us you feel that all you want to do in the cold, wintry start to the year is stay in and hibernate, then use this time to plan your year. You may be tempted to rush down to the January sales to spend your hard earned money on goodies that appeared to be a bargain, but will actually get very little if any use. Think long and hard. Do you really need it, can you actually afford it, and will you ever use it?

January and February are always a good time to have a big clean out and make sure that your tool shed (both DIY and garden) is clean, and your tools sharp and in working order. Check any machinery you may have and service it so that it is in good working order when you need it. Clean down your polytunnel or greenhouse, and make sure that your collection of plant pots and seed trays are thoroughly cleaned and neatly stacked ready for use. We always have a good clean out in the garden as well, or as we like to call it 'slash and burn'. Get rid of all those dead grasses and clippings, and have a cleansing as well as a therapeutic bonfire (if you are allowed to do so). We always buy our seeds in January as they are always on sale at our local garden centre, and keep your eyes peeled for bargains there on things like heated propagators, seed trays, and canes etc. Clear out your vegetable beds and cover them with well rotted horse manure and then sheets of black plastic, and let the worms do their work. Plan your patch and look at what worked well last year and what didn't. In chapter 18 we talked about crop rotation, so be sure to follow these suggestions when planning where to plant your vegetables. Keep the birds well fed with seed mix, peanuts and home-made fat balls too, so they help keep pests down in summer.

March and April are great months because hopefully the cold weather is fading and you are madly sowing your crops (see Chapter G). If like us you use oil-fired central heating, fill your tank up now while prices are cheap. You may want to speak to your neighbours to see if you can organise to get together and bulk order from your supplier to save even more money. Try to keep your beds covered with plastic as this will keep the heat in and help your planting. If you have managed to introduce a pond to help encourage wildlife and insects, now is the time to clean it out. Be careful not to move the fish too much, and if you can use well or rain water to refill the pond it is much kinder to your fish. Ensure you keep it netted otherwise they will become easy pickings for herons. Encourage your compost bins back to life with some compost starter, and keep it regularly mixed and topped up from your kitchen waste.

May and June will really see the garden bearing the fruits of your hard work, so it is important that you get the chance to enjoy it. If you are planning to sell plants and / or vegetables from the roadside, make sure you are ready to do so. Do not obstruct any paths or line of site for drivers, but a couple of small signs printed from your computer and laminated can pre-warn passersby of your little shop! Organise storage space for your excess crops. Make sure the shelving is clean and you have plenty of old jars / containers to keep your produce in. Check freezer storage containers and make sure you have sticky labels.

July and August is the time, if you are fortunate, that most people take their holidays, but don't forget your patch. Try to organise someone to water and feed your fruits and vegetables if you are gone. You can pay them in kind with a basket of goodies from your garden! If you have oil central heating, now is the time to make sure the tank is as full as can be. We find with a 1200 litre tank we can go from August to February on a full tank, and half a tank for the rest of the year. Get your boiler serviced now and ensure it is ready for the winter. If you burn coal or logs, get a store in now when price and demand are low. If you don't buy seasoned logs (which are cheaper), you can buy now for burning the following year as long as you can store them in a dry shed. DIY stores are usually selling off winter stock cheap, so take a look at what's on offer. We live up a steep lane, so we buy our sand and salt mix now, ready for the big freeze.

September and October are the great months of autumn, but there is still lots to plan and think about. If you have open fires, get the chimneys swept. You may want to consider buying a chimney brush attachment for your drain rods and do this yourself. Make sure you lay down plenty of dustsheets and mask the fireplace off with thick plastic and heavy duty duck tape. Check the gutters and downpipes are all clear. You may want to use leftover pieces of chicken wire to cover drains and guttering to prevent them from filling with leaves. Use all those leaves to produce a good free mulch, or store them to make compost (they can take up to 18 months to compost). Depending on the weather, you may now be putting your garden furniture away. Make sure you clean it well and apply teak oil if appropriate. Check your car is serviced and winter ready. You don't want a cracked radiator when the first frosts hit. This is also a good time to change the batteries in your smoke alarm.

November and December see the start of longer, darker nights, and the thought of more time stuck in the house. Make sure all your tools are cleaned and put away securely. Chop some kindling for your open fires, and store it in a sound, dry shed. Check around the outside of your house for any damage that may lead to drafts or a loss of heat, and start to feed the birds ready for winter. Make sure your pond is clear of leaves and dead plants, and try placing a plastic ball in it to help stop the water from freezing. Empty outside water butts to avoid frost damage, and take the netting off the top of your fruit cages so any snowfall does not make them collapse. The garden stores may have started with some good deals on garden equipment, so keep an eye out. Find a source of horse manure, and get a load in ready to spread out in January. You can usually find stables giving it away in the pages of your local paper.

These are just some of the things we plan for on a yearly basis, but we are sure you will have many more ideas of your own. Just spend a little time writing them down and decide when is the best and most economical time to do them. Happy planning!

ZONK!!!

We have now reached the final chapter, and there are not many words beginning with Z to write about. However, we feel that 'Zonk' describes how you may feel sometimes when you are relentlessly working hard at keeping together all the previously mentioned facets of a self-sufficient lifestyle!

Anything worth achieving in life won't be easy, and if it was then everybody would be doing it, but you can take great pride and satisfaction from a hard day's work.

You may find that the more 'glamorous' trinkets of life have become less important than a sense of satisfaction; in our opinion it greatly outweighs any material things we may have given up along the way.

We also hope that you will be feeling healthier and have a greater awareness and control over what you eat. Please don't expect to achieve all your goals and tackle all our suggestions straight away. Use this book more as a reference to help you build a more self-sufficient life over the coming months and years.

We believe that the benefits you should be enjoying will include feeling fitter and healthier, you will be saving money, you will be enjoying life much more, and as your dependency on material things diminishes you will have a much more caring and realistic outlook on life.

We both know from experience that there is nothing to lose, and a huge amount to gain, so enjoy the journey and the new more self-sufficient you.

Times for sterlising fruit using the Cold Bath Method (see page 97)	
Apricots	83°C/180°F 15 minutes
Blackberries	74°C/165°F 10 minutes
Cherries	83°C/180°F 15 minutes
Damsons	83°C/180°F 15 minutes
Gooseberries (for cooking)	74°C/165°F 10 minutes
Gooseberries (for dessert)	83°C/180°F 15 minutes
Peaches	83°C/180°F 15 minutes
Pears	88°C/190°F 30 minutes
Plums	83°C/180°F 15 minutes
Raspberries	74°C/165°F 10 minutes
Strawberries	74°C/165°F 10 minutes

Times for sterlising fruit using the hot water method (see page 97-98)	
Apricots	88°C/190°F 10 minutes
Blackberries	88°C/190°F 2 minutes
Cherries	88°C/190°F 10 minutes
Damsons	88°C/190°F 10 minutes
Gooseberries (for cooking)	88°C/190°F 2 minutes
Gooseberries (for dessert)	88°C/190°F 10 minutes
Peaches	88°C/190°F 20 minutes
Pears	88°C/190°F 20 minutes
Plums	88°C/190°F 10 minutes
Raspberries	88°C/190°F 2 minutes
Strawberries	88°C/190°F 2 minutes

Further Reading

The Fruit Tree Handbook | Ben Pike
Precycle | Paul Peacock
21st Centuray Smallholding | Paul Waddington
How to Store Your Home Grown Produce | J & V Harrison
Making the Most of your Glorious Glut | J Sherman
Practical Self Sufficiency | D & J Strawbridge
The New Complete book of Self-Sufficiency | J Seymour
Booze for Free | Andy Hamilton
The Frugal Life | Piper Terrett
Grow Your Food for Free | Dave Hamilton
The Complete Vegetable Grower | John Harrison
Scenes from a Vegetable Plot | Chas Griffin
Urban Beekeeping | Craig Hughes
The Bee Garden | Maureen Little
The Home Farmer | Paul Heiney
How to Grow Food in your Polytunnel | by M Gatter & A McKay

Magazines

Home Farmer
Smallholder
Country Smallholding
Permaculture

Websites

www.allotment.org.uk
The most popular allotment forum and site in the UK. If you need information it's bound to be here.

www.lowimpact.org
Low-Impact Living Initiative (LILI) is a non-profit organisation whose mission is to help people reduce their impact on the

environment, improve their quality of life, gain new skills, live in a healthier and more satisfying way, have fun and save money.

www.self-sufficientish.com
Thorough useful site and forum about urban self sufficiency.

www.accidentalsmallholder.net
A friendy site and well worth a visit.

www.attainableselfsufficiency.co.uk
Visit our own site for downloads of useful tables and information

The Good Life Press Ltd.
The Old Pigsties, Clifton Fields
Lytham Road, Preston
PR4 0XG
01772 633444

The Good Life Press is a family run business publishing a wide range of titles for the small-holder, 'goodlifer' and farmer. We also publish **Home Farmer,** the monthly magazine for anyone who wants to grab a slice of the good life - whether they live in the country or the city. Other titles of interest:

A Guide to Traditional Pig Keeping by Carol Harris
The A-Z of Companion Planting by Jayne Neville
Ben's Advenures in Wine Making by Ben Hardy
Build It! by Joe Jacobs
Build It!.....With Pallets by Joe Jacobs
Building and Using Your Clay Oven by Mike Rutland
Craft Cider Making by Andrew Lea
Garden Projects for Ruffians by Phil Thane
Precycle! by Paul Peacock
Raising Chickens by Mike Woolnough
The Jammy Bodger by Mel Sellings
The Medicine Garden by Rachel Corby
The Sausage Book by Paul Peacock
The Sheep Book for Smallholders by Tim Tyne
The Smoking and Curing Book by Paul Peacock
Woodburning by John Butterworth
Worms and Wormeries by Mike Woolnough

www.goodlifepress.co.uk
www.homefarmer.co.uk